A BRIDGE OF COMPASSION

A. DONALD MILLER

A
BRIDGE
of
COMPASSION

THE MISSION TO LEPERS
7 BLOOMSBURY SQUARE
LONDON, W.C.1

First Published in 1955
Revised and Enlarged Edition 1960

Printed in England by Wm. Carling & Co. Ltd., London & Hitchin

CONTENTS

CONTENTS

INTRODUCTION TO FIRST EDITION

" I want you to come to one of my bridge parties,"
said the Commissioner of a Division in Northern India
to my missionary friend. It was in the days of the British
Raj; and the missionary had recently gone to live in
those parts.

" Thank you. But I'm sorry, I don't play bridge," said
my friend.

" My dear fellow, I don't mean *that* sort of bridge
party. That's only my little joke. My bridge parties are
affairs I have in my bungalow each week when I invite
people of every description to come and get together—
leaders of the Muslim League, and orthodox Hindus, and
fellows like yourself, and left-wing politicians, and the
college people, and members of the District Council.
We're too much cut off from one another, and what we
need is more bridges to bring us together. Hence my
weekly party."

The Commissioner was right. We need more bridges.
They must contradict and overcome the dividing walls
which men and nations build. Some may be frail and
only fitted for light traffic. But that doesn't invalidate
their usefulness. The many agencies at work which pro-
mote cultural or commercial or artistic intermingling are
of real importance. But stronger and more enduring ones
are needed to bear the strain of heavier traffic, and the
most grievous burdens; and they must be able to resist
the contending currents and tides which swirl about their
supporting piers and strive to undermine them.

7

This short book will tell something of one bridge. It is a bridge made up of the stones of labour and love offered on behalf of men and women and children suffering from leprosy. And especially will these pages tell, from a wholly personal angle of vision, something of the part which The Mission to Lepers has taken and still takes in the building of this bridge. I shall in particular draw on observations, made both during a recent tour of leprosy work which my wife and I made in India and the Far East, and also during the earlier years when we were at work abroad ourselves. If I at times appear to write more about people than about leprosy that is because I am anxious that this work should never be regarded as impersonal; its first and final importance is because it is a work by people for people. It is in this way that it becomes a bridge. It is a bridge which opens up a way for people from bondage to liberty. It brings them healing. It is an instrument of unity and wholeness. It is a Bridge of Compassion.

While I have for convenience divided up this bridge into three arches—the Arch of Physical Healing, the Arch of Human Fellowship, and the Arch of Eternal Hope—I realize that this has its disadvantages. There cannot be any hard and fast division between the varying aspects of Christian leprosy work. It concerns the whole man, and there is not simply an inter-relationship between the physical, social, and spiritual work, but an integration of them into a unity. Nevertheless, if this is remembered, it has seemed to me well to place major emphasis in succeeding chapters upon the part which the medical, social, and religious work have each played, as three arches making up this one strong bridge.

It is unfortunate that this great word " compassion "

has sometimes taken on a sentimental or grandiose flavour. It then savours of condescension, or a rather unintelligent, emotional rushing in to help. Nothing could be further from the real significance of the word. True compassion is a quality unsentimental, costly, practical, efficient. The compassionate man goes out to his neighbour, whatever his need, and stands shoulder to shoulder with him, at hand to help. He does not stoop down to him. He brings succour and friendship and hope because he does not remain superior.

Indeed we do well to remember that the Incarnation itself is the Bridge of God's Compassion. By that Incarnation God built the bridge which issued from His yearning love for men. He got alongside them at their own level, God in man, living and working among men. But at the last even that bridge alone was not enough. Another one which proceeded beyond it was needed. Because of the hardness of men's hearts His compassion had to go on until it became transformed into His own Passion. Having first entered into the sufferings of others He now took them unto Himself, bearing in His own body the sins of all men, though Himself without sin. The Cross was the final bridge.

When my wife and I passed on our recent tour through Japan's old capital city Kyoto we were taken by a hospitable Japanese pastor to a famous old garden. It had been planned many hundred years ago with a profound artistic sensitiveness. And on that frosty, sunlit morning it possessed an almost intoxicating enchantment. In one part of the garden there was a lake, and upon the lake were two islands. I went and stood alone for a time on the farther island looking around upon the fairy-like scene, the winding paths edged with snow, the graceful trees, my friends waiting on the mainland. And then over the two bridges I returned to the company of my host and friends. The first bridge took me to the nearer island, and the second brought me to the shore. I could not but reflect that these bridges were like the Bridge of Compassion and the Bridge of Christ's Passion. While the first took me from my solitariness nearer to my destination, there was still a gulf which required the second bridge. Even so, the Bridge of Compassion needs completion in the Bridge of Christ's Passion. The building of that final bridge is all of God's grace. But in the building of the Bridge of Compassion God calls men to be partners and co-workers. Thus they enter into the work of reconciliation and redemption. And it is of this bridge, in its relevance to a particular situation, that this small book tells.

January, 1955

INTRODUCTION TO REVISED AND
ENLARGED EDITION

Over five years have passed since *A Bridge of Compassion*, in its original form, was written. Now we have entered the seventh decade of the twentieth century, and men's hopes and fears jostle with one another cheek by jowl. We live in a world of greater possibilities for good or evil than ever before. The future all depends upon " where a man's heart is." Scientific, social and economic developments must all contribute either to a better, happier world, or to a more dreadful subjection to the tyrannies of power and ambition.

For those of us who pray " Thy Kingdom come, Thy will be done, on earth as it is in heaven " the challenge of the 1960's is imperatively to take the advances of man's discoveries and offer them back to God in the service of His Kingdom upon earth. So it is that the work of The Mission to Lepers has a strikingly relevant and significant part to play in these days and years when, despite all the advances in the sciences, suffering still abounds. At a time when the twentieth century refugee problem is a bitter and pointed reminder of the product of men's hatred and follies, there is still a danger that the chronic refugee of history, the sufferer from leprosy, may either be forgotten or, if remembered, be regarded and treated in the wrong way. Yet the 'sixties provide unequalled opportunities for grappling with leprosy and all the tortuous human problems which radiate from it. If these opportunities were taken this giant of evil might be

11

mortally wounded in this decade, and dead before the century closes.

In the last five years some of the enterprises described in this book, as originally written, have greatly advanced. Other new ones have begun, especially in Korea and Nepal. Rather than attempt to bring the original manuscript up to date, page by page, it has seemed best to let it stand substantially as it was, and to add a chapter, which appears immediately before the last one, and which I have called The Arches of the Years. This new edition goes out with the hope and prayer that it may win new allies and comrades in the prosecution of a work which brings healing to body, mind and spirit, and helps forward the time when the brokenness of men's fear and hate will be transformed, by the compassion of God at work in men's hearts and hands, into the unity of love.

August, 1960

BEGINNINGS OF THE BRIDGE

I

I begin to write shortly after having returned from a visit to Dublin. I went there to rejoice. With my wife I had been invited to share in celebrations to commemorate an event which took place just eighty years ago. And before I went to the Monkstown Parish Church for the service of thanksgiving there, one lady said to me, " When you're in the pulpit have a good look at the fourth pew back. That is the pew where Charlotte Pim and her sisters used to sit and worship God Sunday by Sunday."

We held the thanksgiving service there at Monkstown on an autumn evening of 1954 because the foundation of The Mission to Lepers owes its origin, humanly speaking, to what followed the hospitality of Isabella, Charlotte and Jane Pim when, in September, 1874, they entertained to tea sturdy and handsome Wellesley Bailey with his young bride, home on furlough from India. The story has often been told of how this young missionary from the Punjab told the sisters of his concern for a handful of mutilated, crippled sufferers from leprosy who lived in a small Leper Asylum at Ambala, one of the very few in India at that time. To his own schoolmastering duties he added this spare-time work of love, going to these men and women and bringing them the cheer of his presence, the little comforts which his purse could afford, and the heart-warming story of Jesus Christ, Son of God, Saviour of men. He talked with them, sang with them, prayed

13

with them. Miss Pim suggested that Mr. Bailey should tell again of this unusual piece of work at a meeting she would arrange at the Friends Meeting House; for though Miss Pim was a member of the Church of Ireland she had many family connections with the Quakers, and many friends among them.

And so the meeting was held; and after it Charlotte said to Wellesley as they walked back home, " We have been thinking that we would like to help in this work, but we cannot promise very much in the way of money; still, we wish to do something, and consider that we could promise, or try to collect, about £30 a year, if such a small sum will be of any real help to you."

In the union of that young missionary's spare-time work at Ambala, and the offering of those sisters in Dublin, The Mission to Lepers of today had its beginning. These sisters could not possibly know what would follow their resolve. Nor could Wellesley Bailey. But they were together laying the first pillar to support a mighty bridge. " You will have to write something for us which we can show to people in order that we can interest them; just put into print what you have been telling us this evening," said the practical Miss Charlotte. So a tiny pamphlet, measuring 4¼ins. by 2¾ins., and bearing the title *Lepers in India,* was produced, and Mr. Bailey, with a hope as big as his heart, sent Miss Pim 2,000 copies, greatly to her consternation. She had thought of 100.

That pamphlet ran through many editions, and came to be known in the Mission as the " Original Beggar ". Instead of £30, the first year produced £527 12s. 10¾d., and the second £809, and the third £936. To what would all this grow?

For nearly four years there was no such thing as a

committee, a constitution, or even a title. There was just a growing group of " friends of the lepers " in Ireland; and back in India once more there was Mr. Bailey, stationed this time up in the Himalayas at Chamba, wondering how he could use the gifts which came to him and which exceeded the need immediately around him. There is an historic entry in the small, unelaborate account book which Mr. Bailey kept. It marked the beginning of the first Home to be built by these eager gifts which reached him.

" May 28th, 1875 : To coolies marking site, 5 annas."

An expenditure of sixpence ! And then, ten months later, when the first row of rooms was ready, this entry for the food costs of the first patient to be admitted : —

" March 31st, 1876 : Ten days' rations for one leper in Chamba, 15 annas 6 pies."

The superstructure above the foundations had begun to appear !

In Dublin the eldest of the three sisters, Miss Isabella Pim, was already something of an invalid, and later became blind; so it was left to Miss Charlotte, the second, to call together, on Mr. Bailey's next return to Ireland in 1878, some of the " friends of the lepers " to discuss what future action should be taken.

I have in front of me a small book of 178 pages, bound in black leather, and bearing on the cover the lettering " Mission to Lepers in India. Minutes of Committee." Its contents cover the proceedings of the committee for fourteen years. It is excellently indexed, and each item of business has its appropriate heading. It begins with a preamble, written in the neat, angular writing of Miss Charlotte : —

COMMITTEE, FIRST FORMATION OF

" There was a meeting of some friends to Indian Lepers held at 28 Westmorland Street Dublin on 26th March 1878, for the purpose of considering the best way of bringing Spiritual and Temporal relief to as many poor outcast Lepers in India as possible, by disposing of the funds already in their hands, and taking steps to collect further means for benefitting these sad sufferers.

" The meeting having been opened with prayer, it was unanimously resolved that Revd. Thomas Good should take the chair."

The meeting elected a committee, chose a title, appointed trustees, planned to open a bank account, determined that at the next meeting (called for only five days later!) the members should get down to the real business of the Mission, and closed with prayer.

Surely a great Society has never been begun with so little fuss and so much faith. Compassion is like that.

II

It was clear to that first committee, made up of four women and five men, that the cause they had embraced was one which could know no narrow national or denominational barriers. Wellesley Bailey, himself a Presbyterian Irishman, had first gone to India with the intention of taking a commission in the Police; and while studying Urdu he lived at Faizabad with a German missionary of an Anglican mission! There he decided to become a lay missionary instead of a policeman; and he received an appointment with an American society. As has already been written, the Misses Pim were members of the Church of Ireland, and the first meeting was held in a Friends Meeting House. Mr. Bailey returned to India as a missionary of the Church of Scotland. So there was already a fine mix-up of nationalities and denominations. The purpose of the committee was simply to seek and follow " the best way of bringing Spiritual and Temporal relief to as many poor outcast Lepers in India as possible ". And so began a work of marvellous co-operation, and soon the Minute Book recorded the response of the Mission to appeals of missionaries of many non-Roman societies, and of various nationalities. It is an interesting commentary that just at the time when Charles Parnell and his colleagues were calling for national independence in their political campaigns, there was this other group of Irish men and women, moved simply with the compassion which Christ had evoked in them, stepping across national boundaries, and ignoring denominational narrowness.

It was not long before abundant use was found for the accumulating funds. Indeed every year a larger volume was required as response was made in faith to all reasonable appeals. The German Lutherans in Eastern India; the American Presbyterians in the Punjab; the Anglicans down in Cochin and up in Kashmir; the British Congregationalists in the Kumaon Hills and down in Travancore; these all figure quite early in the Minute Book. Then came the American Baptists in Burma, the Swiss Reformed in Malabar, the English Baptists in Ceylon. To all these requests response was made. Usually it was for the establishment of new Homes, or the support of efforts already made by individual missionaries. But in the case of the Ceylon request it was for the provision of spiritual ministrations at an old-established government

17

institution. Always the young Mission sought to bring the particular help required, not binding itself down to hard and fast measures.

Very early the committee began to see the need for encouraging separate provision for children of leprosy victims, not themselves infected but running grave risks while they remained with their parents. And it was this encouragement which led to so notable a development of this saving work. It also saw the need to bring before the Government of India the advantages of co-operation, and took the first steps which led to an increasing interest by Government in mission institutions, and then of financial support. It was not until 1886 that Mr. Bailey was invited to become full-time secretary of the Mission. Up till then the increasing burden of work in the gathering and expenditure of funds had been gallantly and quietly borne by the Misses Pim, and the members of the Dublin committee; and it is not until the end of 1887 that Mr. Bailey's writing in the Minute Book takes the place of Miss Charlotte Pim's. The achievement of those early years was one of quite incalculable importance. Foundations had been well and truly laid. And after Mr. Bailey had become secretary he was still strengthened and supported by the undiminished labours of Miss Charlotte Pim. The original committee members also continued to make decisions with broad vision and warm-hearted generosity of spirit, always waiting upon God for His guidance. " The meeting having been opened with prayer " begins the record of meetings, and concludes with " The meeting was closed with prayer." So the work continued to extend and abound. As the Biblical writer was able to attest of God that " His compassions fail not ", so this work of compassion in His name continued with unflagging zeal, and increased with every passing year.

Shorty before her death in 1952 I met again an old lady was was the last survivor of those who had attended that first historic meeting in September, 1874, at the Friends Meeting House in Monkstown. She was now nearly ninety-three and had come to a meeting at which I spoke. " I didn't really hear you," she said to me afterwards, " for I'm very deaf now. But it wouldn't do to give the impression to the younger ones that I've lost my interest and concern, would it?" She was a girl of fourteen when she attended that first meeting, and two years later she became an honorary collector in her district and had carried on for seventy-five years since, even in the frailty of her old age calling on friends to remind them of their privilege of being able to help. " You know," she said to me apologetically, " my list is getting smaller, I'm afraid. So many of my friends have died, and I can't get around as I did and I don't have the same touch with younger people." What splendid loyalty! Hers was a notable example of faithful, quiet discipleship, of Christian faith expressed in compassionate deed. And before she died she had the joy of seeing the beginnings of 1874 grow into a many-arched bridge, across which unnumbered men in their need have passed to a more abundant life.

III

And while friends in Dublin, 5,000 miles away from India, were moved to do something about the plight of impoverished and outcast sufferers from leprosy in that land, there were others who were confronted with this crying need at close range. Some of them were missionaries, some soldiers, others Christian Indians. And they could not just do nothing. " Stealing away is the greatest lying," said Charles Péguy. It is lying because it denies the truth, well understood in the heart, that we are our brother's keeper. But these men and women refused to steal away. Whether by visitation and the friendly word, or by putting their hands into their pockets to give something out of their slender missionary allowances, or by engagement in the direct provision of hospitality, they did something. And God was making provision for them to go forward, once they had proved their faith and their love, through the " friends to Indian Lepers " so far away.

There was a young American doctor at Subathu in the Simla Hills, who on his arrival in 1868 was immediately confronted with the need. " There is no class of the people who have so moved my pity as the lepers in these hills," he wrote. He began to serve them, and when The Mission to Lepers was formed his work was among the very first to be aided. There was young Ensign Ramsey posted by his regiment to the Kumaon hills back in 1835, and his warm heart was at once moved to do what he could. At first it was by almsgiving, and then by the provision of a small house in Almora. But it led to the establishment of the present Almora Home, and the Mission very early in its days began to make maintenance provision for it, and has done so ever since. There also the first organized effort of which record can be found was made to save the children of patients, not yet infected. Two sisters, the Misses Budden of the London Missionary Society, had an orphanage at Almora, and they gladly received these children, and worked for their rescue before ever they were assured of the young Mission's support. And then there followed others, whose open hearts and hands responded to the need around them, without thought of authority from their own missions, or of the financial problems in which their action would involve them. Thus did Haripant Kelkar, Brahmin convert and village schoolmaster, begin to serve at Poladpur; thus did Rosalie Harvey respond to the appeal of starving beggars with leprosy at a time of general famine, and P. A. Penner as he shared his simple fare with other ones at Champa. So did Isobel Hatch in Ramachandrapuram make provision for a servant of hers who contracted the disease, and Dr. Sargood Fry down at Neyyoor for a man full of leprosy who followed him for six miles. From these actions and similar ones by others beginnings were made in faith and compassion, and when that happens God is offered the hands He needs through which to work. And thus great things followed.

It is not possible to pursue this fascinating study of beginnings. But the work as it is today can only be truly understood and appreciated as its pioneer efforts are seen in the background. They proclaim, in deeds that shout louder than words, that compassion is never, never neutral.

In this, the eightieth year of the Mission's history, its

work extends to twenty-four countries; it acts in co-operation with forty-nine missionary societies and the churches which have been established through them*; it sees with gratitude the changing attitudes of governments and peoples from paralyzed fear or indifference to constructive, reasonable service; it gives praise for the many thousands of patients who have found not only a present refuge in their physical need but also an eternal abiding place for their restless souls; it watches and fosters the remarkable medical developments which have synchronized with the growth of the Mission's activities and which are so closely related to them; it thanks God for all those to whom physical relief, and even restoration to full health, have come; and it rejoices that its work has been and remains an instrument of international goodwill and understanding, and of helping forward the day when the Good Shepherd's prayer for His sheep may be fulfilled, that they may become " One Flock, One Shepherd ".

Much, very much, remains to be done, as subsequent pages will make clear. But at the end of this eightieth year we look back and thank God for His faithful pioneers, these men and women of Christ's compassion.

* In 1960, when this revised edition is published, the work extends to 30 countries, and the Mission acts in co-operation with 57 Societies and Churches.

THE ARCH OF PHYSICAL HEALING

I

I fumbled with my earphones in the dimly-lit hall and adjusted the dial to the number which signified English. 1 for Spanish, 2 for French, 3 for English. A doctor from Brazil was speaking in Spanish with great rapidity, and the unseen interpreters could not possibly keep pace or repeat the technical terms swiftly and accurately. When he had finished, a discussion took place from the body of the hall and speakers would begin before the attendants could reach them with microphones. My earphones crackled and spluttered. I gave up trying to follow the debate, removed my earphones, sat back, and let my thoughts roam.

We were in a finely proportioned hall in one of the new university buildings on the edge of Madrid. It was the first week of October, 1953, and we were in session at the sixth International Congress of Leprology. I looked around at the delegates, of whom there were over 300. They had come from countries as far apart as Spain, the U.S.A., the Cameroons, Thailand, Colombia, Syria, Belgium, Kenya, Trinidad, Great Britain, Indo-China, the Philippines, India, Brazil, Malaya, Nigeria, Germany, Turkey, Australia, Madagascar, Peru—to mention but some of them. Outside, the flags of all the countries represented hung from tall white poles, closely clustered together; they waved and rippled against the turquoise blue sky.

A Bridge of Compassion

I turned to the brightly-lit platform. There sat Dr. Muir, doyen of leprologists. He was the secretary-general of the Congress, imperturbable, apparently untirable, perhaps the most selfless man it has been my privilege to know. First a Scottish missionary doctor in Bengal; then the first leprosy research worker at Calcutta; later the servant and friend of various anti-leprosy organizations; always ready to help—at over seventy he returned for The Mission to Lepers to the busy Leprosy Home and Hospital at Purulia in India, to fill an urgent gap; now he is a Vice-President of the Mission, and an active member of Council.

There, too, was Dr. John Lowe, whom I had first known over thirty years ago as a young missionary doctor in India engaged in leprosy work; and since then as one whose unremitting studies have been matched with sound judgment. He was another man who having returned to England after many years of service in India, went out to meet an urgent need in Nigeria, and engaged in some of the most striking clinical research work upon the treatment of leprosy by the sulphone drugs. At the side of the chairman of the session was Dr. H. W. Wade, a man as loyal as he is thorough and far-seeing, who when the Japanese came to the Philippines stood by his thousands of leprosy patients upon the lonely island of Culion, refusing the opportunity given him to leave, and electing to share with the patients any new unknown hardship which might be theirs. At a later stage of the meeting Dr. Robert Cochrane took over the chairmanship, and my mind went back to the day when I had greeted him on Ballard pier at Bombay in November, 1924, a fresh medical missionary recruit, come to devote himself to leprosy work; and a man who from that day to this has

24

laboured like a Trojan, wrestling with the problems of the disease, and approaching all his work with an inflexible Pauline conviction that Christ has commissioned him to this task. There, on that platform, three out of the four whom I knew were men who had gone out as medical missionaries; and the other was a man of great compassion. All were bridge-builders. Their years of brilliant work had placed them where they were and enabled them to speak with authority and be undisputed leaders in the world of leprology.

How wonderful it was that there was now this great gathering, at which the majority of delegates were not medical missionaries, but state or university representatives. They proclaimed how far advance has been made in recent years by governments and peoples to take an increasing share of the load of anti-leprosy activity. Indeed, the medical missionary in some cases has now changed his rôle from that of pioneer to partner, supplying the dynamic enthusiasm and Christian conviction which enables him to engage with greatest success in the daily care of multitudes of simple people.

As I watched Dr. Muir contributing to the debate I recalled how at the smaller Congress at Cairo in 1938 he had said at its opening in the red-plush-seated Opera House, with the young King Farouk present, that leprosy was the Cinderella of diseases. That was certainly no longer true now. Increasing attention has been given to it, and one does not have to search far to find the tributes of government ministers and officials to the essential part played by Christian missions in creating this change. The initial thrust of compassion effected the altered approach from fear to love, and set in motion constructive as distinct from merely protective action. True, the changed medical situation which took leprosy out of the dark realm of untreatable diseases has had its important effect. But that change is itself in considerable measure due to the part which Christian missionaries, of whatever church allegiance, took in relating the laboratory probings and speculations and findings of scientists to the needs and hopes of leprosy victims who found in Christian missionaries their readiest friends.

It is, for instance, of great significance that the story of Father Damien's action to go and live among an unloved, banished company of sufferers on a lonely island in the Pacific, there to contract the disease and see it develop in its most serious form, focused attention on the leprosy problem not only in the Hawaii islands, but also within the British Empire, and particularly India. Under the Presidency of H.R.H. the Prince of Wales— later King Edward VII—a group was constituted in 1889, only three months after Father Damien's death, " to consider the best way of perpetuating his memory ". A fund was created which enabled a representative Commission to proceed to India the following year to engage in a widespread investigation. As they travelled they found again and again that it was missionaries who were doing what they could to meet the problem at the point of individual need, and the Report pays tribute to these men and women " who spared no trouble in rendering every possible assistance ". The Commission arrived at certain important conclusions, though some have later been shown to be wrong. One of the positive and important practical conclusions was that leprosy was *not* hereditary. A reason why the Commission contradicted the theory was that they found evidence that where children of parents with leprosy were separated from them while quite young they did not contract the disease; and it was in this work of faith that The Mission to Lepers had in its early days so important a part to play. It is also interesting to read the notes which the Commission made on efforts to provide curative treatment. It commented on gurjun oil, which had been tried in the Andaman Islands, and which Wellesley Bailey very early in his work noted and tried; and also on chaulmoogra oil, long reputed in the East to give good results, so long as its nauseating flavour could be tolerated. " It seems that the action of chaulmoogra oil in leprosy, though at the best palliative, is nevertheless more marked than that of gurjun oil."

Another instance of the influence of Christian missions on the development of work for the care of leprosy victims and the wiping out of the disease is in the formation of The British Empire Leprosy Relief Association in 1923. When the Rev. Frank Oldrieve was the Secretary for India of The Mission to Lepers he aroused, by brilliant and well-directed effort, a sudden increase of practical interest in high circles, based directly upon what was being attempted at the Mission's Homes in India, and upon the new medical hope engendered by leprosy research work at the School of Tropical Medicine, Calcutta, and its clinical application at such large Homes of the Mission as the one at Purulia in Bihar. Sir Frank Carter, a Christian business man, and one with a heart full of compassion, gave much encouragement. Sir Leonard Rogers of the Indian Medical Service entered enthusiastically into the promotion of this new body. The possibility of a great effort to rid the British Empire of leprosy was conceived, in which all men of goodwill, extending beyond the range of those directly identified with Christian missions, should have a share. And so it was, with Mr. Oldrieve becoming the first secretary of the new organization, that this body was created. In the years that have followed, it has done much, and especially in British colonies in Africa, to develop constructive effort to eradicate the disease. I recall with what trepidation I, as a young and inexperienced missionary expecting my life's work to be at a single Leprosy Home, was suddenly instructed to step into the old shoes which Mr. Oldrieve swiftly loosed when the new call came to him. Inexperienced as I was, I was glad that I was available at the time to relieve Mr. Oldrieve of his former position, so that he could engage in another pioneer work which has since so signally shared in the building of the arch of healing in this bridge of compassion.

II

It is neither necessary, nor possible, to trace the stages by which knowledge about leprosy and its treatment increased. This great change has come during the eighty years of The Mission to Lepers' work. Up till the time of the Mission's establishment it may be said that leprosy, so ancient a disease, had pursued its sinister, destructive way through the centuries, broadening the area of its depredations with the movements of peoples and increase of world population. From Africa and the East it spread into Europe. By the nineteenth century it had died down in those European countries which had the greatest urban populations, but remained firmly, if not heavily, entrenched in countries with more rural isolated populations like Norway. Indeed, there was such a dangerous increase of leprosy in Norway in the middle of the nineteenth century that it led to the first real effort to study the disease scientifically. The Norwegians Danielssen and Boech certainly arrived at some wrong conclusions, coming to the view that leprosy was hereditary and not contagious. But Dr. Armauer Hansen, at Bergen, discovered early in the 1870's (some say 1871, others 1872 or 1873) that the cause was a bacillus, the *mycobacterium leprae*. This created a revolution in approach to the disease. Old ideas died slowly—the curse of the gods; hereditary transmission; or wild ideas about infection from food and so on—these all persisted and to some degree still persist in unenlightened circles. But now that it was known by scientists that the cause was a bacillus the ultimate goal was to destroy it wherever it could be found, and meanwhile prevent as far as possible its transmission from victim to healthy person, either by compulsory or voluntary segregation, or the removal of healthy children. A new hope was born; and it is surely remarkable that it was precisely at this time of discovery that Wellesley Bailey was paying his first visits to the leprosy sufferers at Ambala, about which he spoke to those friends in Dublin when he returned to Ireland in September, 1874. It was also in May, 1873, that Father Damien went first to Molokai to live among the malodorous, uncared-for victims there. These early years of the 1870's mark the silent passage of midnight for the world's victims of leprosy. A new day was beginning, though the visible dawn would be some time before it appeared.

During the years that have followed knowledge has slowly increased and there has been again and again a strange (or is it not strange?) conjunction of compas-

C

sionate action and scientific advance. For instance, an important discovery was made by a Japanese doctor, Dr. Kensuke Mitsuda, which makes it possible for the degree of resistance to leprosy in an individual to be measured. It was my privilege to meet him only in February, 1954, still busy at his work at the Nagashima Leprosarium, the man who has given the longest service of any doctor in the world to leprosy work, for he began in 1898, and has a record now of fifty-seven years' continuous service.

How did he come to engage in this labour? The answer is substantially, if indirectly, to be found in the large-hearted compassion of a woman missionary to Japan, Miss H. Riddell. Living at Kumamoto she saw the plight of leprosy sufferers there. In the whole of Japan there was only one small Leprosy Home, at Shizuoka, founded by a Father Tostwonide in the year Father Damien died, 1889. Miss Riddell wrote to The Mission to Lepers in 1893, " Kind as the Japanese are to suffering generally, it is a very usual supposition that leprosy is not a disease according to the law of nature; and having no natural cure, those afflicted by it cannot therefore be of the same order of humanity as others. It would seem that for the lepers there is no hope either in this world or the next, *unless we take it to them.*"

In the following year The Mission to Lepers made a capital grant to her, and thus encouraged she determined to build a Home. This set in motion unexpected developments. Soon another lady, Miss Youngman at Tokyo, was asking for help, and the Mission responded; and a Home managed from the beginning by Christian Japanese was opened. It was called significantly Ihaien, meaning Garden of Comfort for the Outcast. But interest went much further. Miss Riddell's work in particular was noticed in royal and high government circles. Provincial governments were quickened into activity; and so it was that Dr. Mitsuda commenced his work at the Yoku-in Hospital in Tokyo. All leprologists throughout the world are indebted to him for the "Mitsuda lepromin test". This has now come to have an even additional potential value in relation to the B.C.G. vaccine, which may prove to have prophylactic value against leprosy as well as tuberculosis. Thus the small beginnings in compassionate act led to striking rapid developments, so that today Japan has twelve national Leprosaria with over 10,000 patients being well cared for in them.

When I saw Dr. Mitsuda in his own study at Naga-shima, with its rather Edwardian furnishings upholstered in brown velvet, he was busily engaged in microscopic work at a window which looked out upon the Inland Sea. He is now over eighty; but wearing no glasses he was busily setting down with fine brushes, on to a circle of paper at his side, the picture of a leprosy "section" which he saw through the lens. He has made thousands of such pictures, and his recently published *Atlas of Leprosy,* with its brilliant coloured plates of leprosy sections, is a monumental work. As I stood by Dr. Mitsuda I noticed a large card with beautiful Japanese writing on it. I commented on its charm and asked its meaning. At once Dr. Mitsuda smilingly presented it to me. It was in his own calligraphy and was a prayer that there might rest upon his work the grace and compassion of a notable figure in old Japanese story. He, too, was a mighty bridge-builder.

With increased knowledge the search for a treatment became more intensive. In 1905 an Egyptian began to give chaulmoogra oil by injections, but it was not until the second decade of the century that others began to adopt this method, which cut out all the nauseating effects of oral administration. And then, thirty years later, came another leap forward with the advent of the sulphone drugs. In them, it may be said, workers on the treatment of tuberculosis paid back, abundantly, the debt they owed to this discovery by Hansen of the causative bacillus of leprosy, for he made his discovery some years before Kock discovered the causative bacillus of tuberculosis, and in this he was helped by Hansen's work and technique.

The basic sulphone (4,4'-diamino-diphenyl sulphone, as the chemists call it) was first synthesized by German workers as far back as 1908. But it was not until 1937 that both French and British workers separately found that this diamino-diphenyl sulphone (or D.D.S.—and sometimes D.A.D.P.S.—as it is known for short) was active against certain micro-organisms. Then followed an experiment in 1940 by Rist in France which showed that D.D.S. was able to inhibit the growth of tubercle bacilli. Now the causative bacillus of tuberculosis has certain characteristics in common with the *mycobacterium leprae,* and therefore the leprosy research worker always watches with eagerness any advances in the treatment by drugs of tuberculosis. The fact therefore that D.D.S. inhibited the growth of tubercle bacilli was a signal for leprologists to be on the alert. But because of insufficient knowledge of D.D.S. it fell into disfavour and only derivatives came to be used in its place. Leprologists, especially in the U.S.A. at first, began to use these derivatives, which were costly, and which gave some encouraging results. But in time the parent sulphone (D.D.S.)

came into use again about the year 1947. It was then given in cautious, tiny doses, and was found to be effective, and at a price immensely less than that of the derivatives. So it began to be possible to give treatment at a cost (so far as the drug went) of less than ten shillings a year. The opportunity of treatment on a wide scale entered the horizon.

III

I turned around in the Congress Hall, from which in these reflections we have wandered so far, to see who was sitting behind me, and found it was Dr. A. R. Davison, whom I had last met nearly four years previously at the Westfort Institution, Pretoria. Then he had shown my wife and me this great Leprosy Institution maintained by the government of the Union of South Africa. He had, among other interesting things, shown me photographs of Dr. George Turner as he was when he also had engaged in work at Westfort. In Sir George Turner was one more medical pioneer who was quickened by compassion to add to his major research work on rinderpest the task of doing something to lighten the darkness which surrounded the means by which leprosy is transmitted. Dr. Turner had his theories; and in his experimental work he unhappily contracted the disease himself; and before his death His Majesty King Edward VII showed the honour in which he held him for his sacrifice by making him a Knight. The visitor to the Parish Church of Hoddesdon in Hertfordshire may find a plaque to his memory on the north wall.

But it was another incident which I recalled as I saw Dr. Davison. We had been passing down a road of the

Institution when we came near to the carpenters' shop, staffed by patients. " In the old days," said Dr. Davison, " they put over the door their own chosen sign—a signboard with a coffin on it. Always they were making coffins for their fellow-patients as they died. But now all that is changed. With the coming of the sulphone drugs we don't get so many deaths; we get discharges instead. And so the carpenters have taken down their sign and put up another one."

" What is it?" I asked.

" Look and you'll see; it's a greyhound straining at the leash, eager to be off."

How that change reflected the new surging hope which came with the sulphone drugs! But all those hopes have not been realized. There is great improvement of symptoms; after long, steady, skilled treatment, there is even more, a destruction of the hosts of bacilli. But many cases have not even yet, after years of treatment, reached that ultimate goal of complete freedom from the disease.

So I turned to Dr. Davison and said, " Have they still got the sign of the greyhound straining at the leash?"

" No," he said sadly. " They've taken it down, and haven't one now. But I know what they ought to have —a tortoise!"

That was a significant and good answer. The Sign of the Tortoise. Slow but sure.

Later, at the closing session of the Congress, Dr. Muir said:—

" If a patient comes early for treatment, in practically every case we can assure him that the disease is not likely to advance. It may take years to get better, but if he has not become an advanced case he will not have to leave his work and he has every prospect of getting better in the end."

And then he closed with these significant words : —

" I believe that, although we wish to carry on research into better drugs, we have at hand already enough means to stamp out leprosy. One thing is wanted and that is the right kind of doctor and nurse, and once we have these I believe this problem will cease to exist as a problem."

So there we are, back at the personal factor. The need is for trained men and women with a sense of vocation eager and equipped to go to the multitudes of untreated leprosy victims in the world today. There are not less than five million of them*. Many of the stones for the arch of healing are at hand, albeit they still need cutting more perfectly into shape. It is the masons who are required.

IV

But even with medicines and with men this does not meet the whole physical need of the leprosy sufferer. It is one of the tragic ironies of the disease that the person who having contracted the disease thereafter shows *most* resistance to the bacilli, is the very person who is most prone to the greatest crippling and disfiguring effects. Do not expect me to describe clearly the reasons for this strange fact. But I think I would be right in saying (in admittedly much over-simplified language) that just

* Note to Revised Edition, 1960. The World Health Organisation gives an estimate of between ten and twelve million at the end of 1959. Vide W.H.O. Chronicle, January 1960.

because there is strong resistance the invading bacilli find it hard to spread easily and widely throughout the body. They therefore entrench themselves in what we may call outposts near to nerves which record sensation from and impulses to the skin. Here their pressure in time renders the nerves ineffective, and lack of sensation follows. Injuries through burns and knocks, unrecognized at the time because of lack of sensation, follow. Slowly the bacilli come to invade the superficial nerve trunks, especially those which supply impulses to fingers and toes. Hands and feet gradually become clumsy and crippled; the typical " claw hand "—half closed and unable to open— appears. The small bones of fingers and toes become frail and may in time be absorbed. Infection may also occur as a result of injury leading to still further destruction of tissue. Stumps alone remain in the final state if no earlier arrest has been made. And all this time the victim may remain quite healthy in himself. He is now referred to as suffering from the *tuberculoid* type of the disease. Popularly he has usually been spoken of as suffering from the neural type. It must of course be remembered that every tuberculoid case does not advance until the worst consequences are evident; indeed, such cases constitute a minority of the total, for in many instances the infection remains mild.

The man who contracts leprosy and has *less* resistance is subject to other manifestations and consequences of the disease. He is known to be suffering from leprosy in its *lepromatous* form. The invasion of bacilli, because less strongly opposed, becomes deeper and more widespread. The skin becomes elevated into nodules, in which millions of bacilli may be found. The face sometimes takes on a leonine expression. As the disease advances, severe fever, or " lepra reaction "—a kind of frenzied effort to resist—takes place. Health declines; and the victim does not normally continue to live on into old age, as many purely tuberculoid cases do.

Between this " polarization " of the two major directions in which leprosy develops there are intermediate, or mixed forms; and there is sometimes a period of what one might call irresolution—" to be or not to be, that is the question "—when it is not clear which way the disease will leap, towards the tuberculoid or the lepromatous form, or to a spontaneous cure. At this stage the disease is often classified at " borderline ".

Among sufferers from the tuberculoid form of leprosy there are hundreds of thousands of men and women, and even young people, who before ever they can receive benefit from sulphone treatment suffer those neural injuries which result in crippling and deformity. For such injuries the sulphones can do nothing. The marks, the awkward movements, the lack of sensation, remain. And those who suffer these penalties are stigmatized as " lepers ", even though all active disease may cease. A fire in a building dies out, or is quickly extinguished by the advent of the fire brigade and well-directed hose-pipes, but charred remains are left where the flames have already done their work of destruction. The fire brigade and the fountains of water can do nothing about them. So with leprosy. Sulphones can do little or nothing to restore nerves already severely damaged to the extent of producing deformity. What they can do is to prevent further advance of the disease, contain it, and thus minimize deformity; or, if it has not yet appeared, prevent it. That is great gain. But it is not everything.

What can be done for the folk who have suffered

nerve injury? In Leprosy Homes, before the days of treatment—and even now—they came to be the ones who because of their deformities and the fear of the community to receive them back into normal social life increasingly occupied available space and used up financial resources. Yet how could they be discharged, without that discharge virtually sentencing many of them to social ostracism and exiled beggary?

For many years, often in an unscientific, empirical way, Homes tried to do what they could to minimize or delay deformity. Patients would be encouraged to massage one another with oil and engage in simple finger-extension exercises, or work at occupations to stimulate finger movements. While I worked in India I saw physiotherapy departments established at two large Leprosy institutions, Dichpalli in Hyderabad and Chandkhuri in what is now Madhya Pradesh. At Dichpalli, Dr. Isobel Kerr was one of the pioneers in this direction. She was a very remarkable woman, possessed not only of rare skill as a doctor, but also of a serenity which seemed almost to emanate from her, bringing peace to others, and establishing a new atmosphere of calm wherever she moved. Certainly this serenity, born of a deep Christian faith, enabled her so to be at the disposal of her Master that she was able to carry through an enormous amount of work each day, which most people could not have done. Free from inner conflicts and frustrations, her whole energy was used for others' gain. I remember sitting with her in a train from Secunderabad to Dichpalli, far away back in 1924. The journey gave her opportunity for a few hours to rest from her labours. She had just finished a morning at the leprosy clinic at Hyderabad City, a pioneer one, for at that time they were extremely rare. After reaching Dichpalli she would have an evening medical round to make at the leprosy hospital which she and her husband had established. It was hot and dusty, and she might well have rested for that four-hour journey. But almost at once she got out some pieces of wood from a bag, assembled them as a small loom and began to work. When I asked her what she was making she told me that she was only just learning, teaching herself to weave three-inch wide strips of coarse cotton, in order that she might set some of her patients to work, for the benefit of their fingers. It was the first thought-out experiment of its kind I had seen. As I think of that journey now, I realize with what prophetic insight and understanding Dr. Kerr worked.

If the reader will suffer me to make a brief digression, I would like, because it is a commentary on the theme of this book, to refer to the beginnings of Mr. and Mrs. Kerr's work, for they have a special interest in view of the fact that today the Dichpalli Leprosy Home and Hospital is one of the most notable and successful ones in India. Back in 1911 there are references in The Mission to Lepers' magazine, *Without the Camp*, to the need in the Hyderabad State, and to Dr. Kerr and a lady colleague trying out a German drug called nastin on leprosy sufferers who appealed for help.

Mr. Kerr wrote from Nizamabad:—

"Only this morning a villager came from a place twenty miles off. He was quite prepared to stay if there were any hope of getting the new medicine of which he had heard. As to clinical results of the nastin I am afraid our medical ladies are not greatly enthusiastic. . . ."

And later followed an appeal from Mr. Kerr to enable him and his wife to start a small residential Home. The Mission made an encouraging response.

" Your hopefulness cheers us. The prospects of our leper work were never brighter—the people coming so regularly, and appealing to us for shelter, but the outlook so far as the buildings are concerned seems darker than ever."

So The Mission to Lepers made a substantial initial grant for buildings, and soon temporary structures were erected, and later the present Home at Dichpalli, owned by the Methodist Missionary Society. When Mr. Kerr knew that he could go forward he was able on his preaching tours to encourage the neediest sufferers that soon they might find Christian hospitality. Movingly, he wrote of one man :—

"A little way off, yet well within hearing distance, sat a man whose very attitude betokened a leper. Poor fellow, he was without fingers and toes, but he had all the soul of a man looking out of his eyes, and I could see he was eager to hear these new truths. I sat down near him and told him of the Healer and Saviour of lepers. The story of the Saviour able to save to the uttermost had a wonderful effect on my hearer. I could see the light of a new hope dawn on him. That God cared for him, and loved him, and that He assured him of His love by the death of His Son was a gospel indeed to the poor man. The dread disease, he thought, put him outside the pale of all spiritual, as it does most social, privilege. It was not for him, this light and love that already was changing the hearts of the people around him. God's curse was upon him, and not His love. How could God care for him, when He sent this trouble to rob him of his wife and children, friends and home? These questionings found ready expression, for he was eager to know if even for him there was even now a Saviour. Afterwards, when I told him that shortly I should take him away from all the shunning and abhorrence of old friends and from dependence on their grudging bounty and should care for him and tell him more of Him Who restoreth our souls, his joy was very real indeed."

Great faith was shown there by that missionary in telling an outcast man without fingers and toes that Christ was " able to save to the uttermost ". But how the years have justified that faith! I shall later be writing of the directly spiritual arch of this bridge of compassion; and for the time it must suffice to remind ourselves by this passage that the greatest need was met by word of the greatest solace in that touching conversation. What I would immediately emphasize is that it was the active faith of Mr. and Mrs. Kerr, and the co-operation of unnamed friends in different parts of the world in their gifts to The Mission to Lepers, that constituted the beginning of the building up of an institution which pioneered physiotherapy in India for leprosy patients, a work which has made a sudden recent advance through the skill, devotion and imagination of a man about whom I now want to write, Paul Brand.

V

Paul Brand wanted to become a missionary, as his father had been. And he wanted to use his hands as well as his tongue. It did not then seem possible for him to become a doctor, and he therefore trained to be a builder, working with masons, and also learning planning and costing of buildings. But the way opened for him to engage in medical studies and he trained in London, and qualified during the first half of the last war. Surgery attracted him, and the war gave him unusual opportunities, while delaying the realization of his desire to become a missionary doctor. In particular, orthopædic surgery drew his interest. He always marvelled at the beauty, and the amazingly delicate mechanism of hands, their sensitiveness and their strength, the perfect way in which impulses were conveyed from brain to hand, and sensations from hand to brain. So he engaged in special study of the hand, and its care.

The war ended, Paul took his English Fellowship of the Royal College of Surgeons, and in time opportunity came for him to go out as an orthopædic surgeon to the Vellore Christian Medical College in South India, and as associate professor in orthopædics.

It was then that Dr. Robert Cochrane took him to see the leprosy settlement in Chingleput, seventy or eighty miles away. There Dr. Cochrane had during many years done a great work as a physician; and his research work, especially in leprosy as it affected children, was quite outstanding. He had become a Fellow of the Royal College of Physicians, as Dr. Brand had become a Fellow of the Royal College of Surgeons. The two missionaries walked around among the many hundreds of patients. Paul saw the crippled hands, so twisted, so ineffective. Hands that had once been beautiful, sensitive. It shook him. Could his special skill and knowledge bring some measure of restoration, that they might become working hands again? Would tendon transplantations be possible?

" I'm no surgeon," said the physician, " but I can tell you that the tissues of leprosy patients heal well, after minor operations, and if you think you can transplant tendons and re-shape bones to turn these miserable beggars into useful citizens, it's just what I've been wanting to do for years."

So the surgeon began his task with volunteers who knew he couldn't make their hands worse, and perhaps might make them better. Some good results followed. But after that, what? Paul Brand was not just a surgeon who might say, " Now I've done *my* job; the rest is for others." He was a man before he was a surgeon, a Christian before he was a doctor. And he was a practical man, a Christian workman. At his building work he had learned to use the tools of carpenter and mason. And so there came into being another venture of inestimable significance, the training of men, healed of active leprosy, but handicapped with hand injuries and deformities which had been partially restored by surgery, to engage in occupations which would enable them to become self-supporting citizens instead of beggars, and have the right at least to claim a place as citizens in the general community, whatever the general community might do about it.

But again, the missionary needed some financial resources; not great ones; indeed, Dr. Brand from the first sensed the danger of establishing anything which would divorce patients from the sort of simple setting in which the rest of their lives must obviously be lived. But he needed *some* finances. And then, as had so often happened before, the compassion of one was met by the compassion of another; " one loving heart sets another on fire "; the young man found in an old lady his partner to help him in beginning to build. She was a patient at the College Hospital. This is how Dr. Brand describes her : —

"Then came Mother Eaton.

" She had come to us because of her arthritis in the hope that we could relieve her of some of her pain. We found to our disappointment that there was nothing very dramatic that we could do for her, that she would have to go on with a good deal of the old pain, with the slight relief of a few pills and injections.

43

" Pain makes some people hard and bitter, but where the grace of God is, it often seems to bring out a greater love and sympathy. While Mother Eaton was sleepless with pain, she was thinking about our leper patients that she had heard about the previous day, and thinking too about some money that she had put aside to build a Christian village for the poor.

" In the morning she told us about her idea. ' Put up some huts in village style, and let your cured patients live there as a little community centred around a training shed where they will learn to become self-supporting. After a few months they can go on to their own villages and make room for some more.'

" Mother Eaton gave us enough money to start to build, and the first huts are now complete and the first trades are being taught, and before long the first of the men will be ready to go out and face the world as soon as we are able to give them a start in their home villages. We do not expect the Rehabilitation Centre to grow very big. We wish rather that it shall accommodate a succession of patients who will each stay only a few months and go out with new life.

" The name of the Centre in Tamil means the ' Place of New Life ', and we want it to be just that—new life physically, mentally, and spiritually, and we want also the way of this new life to be learnt by others throughout the world who are working for those who suffer from this disease."

I visited that Centre in December, 1953. With my wife I had gone to Vellore to take part in the dedication of the first major buildings of the Schieffelin Leprosy Research Sanatorium at Karigiri, seven miles out in the country. And while we were there, Dr. Brand, now a colleague on the direct missionary staff of The Mission to Lepers, and director of its orthopædic work, took us to the New Life Centre, on the far side of the city. It was one of the great experiences of my life. On the way

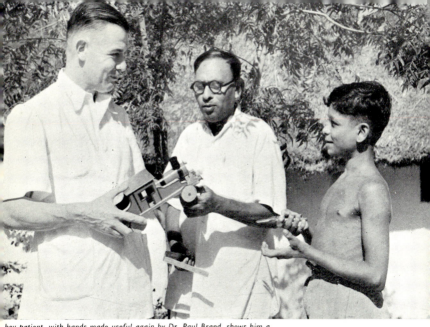

boy patient, with hands made useful again by Dr. Paul Brand, shows him a
y engine he has learned to make

THE NEW LIFE CENTRE, VELLORE, SOUTH INDIA

Finger drill for young men crippled with tuberculoid leprosy.   See pages 41–47

A NEW LEPROSY RESEARCH SANATORIUM

Left: *Dr. Ida Scudder cuts the first sod at Karigiri, Vellore, September, 1952*

Centre: *The Research Block going up, Spring, 1953*

Below: *Completed staff houses at the foot of Elephant Hill, December, 1953.*
See pages 54–57

we had called at the leprosy out-patient clinic at the hospital, and had seen Dr. Brand's staff, led by Dr. Fritschi, engaged in their work. My wife became absorbed in watching the techniques used; the tests for nerve response; the wax baths; the finger exercises, with the well-initiated patients teaching the newer ones; the photographs and records. Here much was being done to bring to patients with minor deformity the means by which they would be saved from suffering the more severe contractures, or losses of fingers. Work was also being engaged in on feet, of only second importance to that on hands.

The " Place of New Life " to which we motored on from the clinic was indeed a garden of resurrection. A first glimpse of it showed neat mud-walled buildings, whitewashed and with grass-thatched roofs over which sprawled the lovely blue convolvulus-like flower called morning glory. Besides the paths poinsettias with their petal-like vermilion leaves were in bloom. The buildings were set pleasantly together, compact but not crowded, and one of them was a simple church, made of the same materials as the other buildings, and largely the labour of a group of Christian university students, particularly from the Christian College at Tambaram, who made this labour of love a vacation enterprise. We were taken to the operating theatre, so dramatically in contrast to the white-tiled operating rooms of the Vellore Christian Medical College Hospital, with their bewildering array of gleaming modern instruments and appurtenances. Here Mr. Brand (let us speak of him here in the traditional manner of surgeons) had contrived inexpensive alternatives to the costly equipment of the modern hospital. For instance, he had made a shadowless lamp for

45

D

just one-hundredth of the cost of the catalogued article —Rs.30 instead of Rs.3,000! A metal disc reflector had been beaten out into concave shape, polished, and suspended by a series of intricate and yet simple pulleys to the ceiling. One could move it with complete precision to any position; and with the necessary electric bulb it did all the work required of it. A solar heater to make distilled water was being experimented with, so that instruments might be sterilized in distilled and not ordinary water, which helps greatly to preserve the perfect edge of knives.

We went on to the workshop and saw a busy, happy, smiling group of men busily at work. All of them had more or less crippled hands, but they were now useful and trained hands. Special tool-holders had been made for them, so that even without the full use—for instance —of thumbs they could yet use scissors with special handles. Jigsaw puzzles were being cut; Chinese chequerboards were being made and coloured; a gay array of painted toys was shown to us. The workers laughed with us as we delighted in the antics of a painted jester who went somersaulting down a slope. Experimental work on making plastic containers was being engaged in. Mr. Brand's aim is to train these men to engage in crafts or occupations which they can carry through *alone*; for in the average community they will not be able to join in team work, not so much from inability as from the social prejudice which confronts them. Marketing is a matter calling for attention, and also the development of one-man industries which deal with the basic requirements of a village rather than with those extras of life which one may buy in a city shop if one has the means. There is still a vast field of experimental work ahead. To me the inspiration of the project was that here was a community of men with hitherto useless hands, now conforming to a proper time-schedule of work, learning and labouring together, filled with new hope, able to look forward to a day when they might become self-supporting. This sort of thing has been done, of course, in other settings and circumstances, as at the notable Papworth Village in England for patients healed of tuberculosis. But for men healed of leprosy, yet still crippled by its effects, this was something new and notable.

Such a work is one which calls very specially for the concern and support of those who hold an ardent faith in the value of the individual. Dr. Brand himself has pointed out that while such work as his cannot in any way control the disease, it has a special claim on those who are builders of the Bridge of Compassion.

"We have known patients with crippled hands who have no outside resources, who dread the day when their skin test will become negative, and who will even bribe the technician to show a false positive result, so that they may be kept in the sanatorium and saved from the life of roadside begging, which is their only alternative. We, as a Christian missionary medical organization, should regard this type of case as being one of our first responsibilities, and use all our influence to resist the idea that a patient may be lightly discharged as 'cured' when his physical disabilities are such as to give him no hope for the future."

VI

Bearing this in mind, and acting accordingly as best we may, we must at the same time also recognize the importance of the work of bringing the benefits of treat-

47

ment to the very early cases of leprosy; and also of the work of prevention. It is now more clearly realized that very soon after infection has taken place irreparable neural injury often occurs, though the crippling effects may not be seen for years. It is therefore of quite vital importance to bring the benefits of sulphone treatment to leprosy victims at the earliest possible moment. I have just received, even as I write this, a report from Dr. Edwards on the staff of The Mission to Lepers' Home at Moulmein in Burma, who in addition to his institutional duties has recently made an examination of 4,000 children in the local schools. He found that between one and two per cent of them already had early signs of the disease, a shockingly large proportion unless treatment could be provided for them *at once*. In some of the schools the teachers were co-operating in seeing that the sulphones were given, without otherwise disturbing the children's life. That particular illustration makes clear both the seriousness of the situation and its hopefulness where swift and enlightened measures are taken.

It is clear that widespread work in early diagnosis and treatment, and in educational work on social hygiene as applied to leprosy, can only be successfully undertaken by the comprehensive organization of public health services in those lands where leprosy still constitutes a major problem. No mission, no private, locally-stationed organization, can cover work of this kind. What it can do is to work intelligently in limited local circumstances, hoping that the work will be taken up in a wider way by public authorities, as the value of it is recognized. This is what has happened, quite notably, in the Owerri Province of Nigeria. In the 1920's and 1930's missions pioneered; then government came to co-operate with them; in time it became the major partner, with medical missionaries continuing to be the most valuable executives; finally government came to recruit its own leprosy service personnel, but still found among its best members doctors of missionary experience. As the years passed the institutional approach came to be supplemented by out-patient work; then by village segregation centres and by rural treatment clinics; a whole network of activities developed by which, more and more, the early case was both discovered and treated, and the general public were increasingly protected. From the institution and the advanced case the emphasis has passed to the village and the early case. The results have been the most encouraging ones in Africa. While other factors have contributed to the good results—as for example a higher natural resistance to the disease than among, say, people in India or Burma—yet it is largely due to the measures I have described, and the swing in emphasis and energy, that in this Province the problem of leprosy is being definitely overcome. The arch of healing is being brought to completion, and the way of liberty from a great enemy opened up, to the benefit not only of this generation but of all the future.

It was my privilege to see something of rather similar, if at present less developed, work of this kind in the South Arcot Division of Madras, just after I had seen the " Place of New Life " at Vellore, which is itself in North Arcot. In this Division there has been a striking development in recent years of work hitherto engaged in for the most part by Christian organizations, but now increasingly undertaken by national bodies. Once again one finds the spark of constructive action in the compassionate heart. It is a story that Professor Jagadisan

49

has permitted me to set down, for he is too big a man
to claim my silence over the personal circumstances
which brought him into leprosy work as an ardent and
successful leader. As a young professor of English at
the Annamalai University he had come greatly under
the personal influence of that remarkable Indian states-
man, Srinivasa Sastri. The liberal and large-hearted
sympathies of that leader fired young Jagadisan with a
burning patriotism, as did his simple life as one of that
small and distinguished band of workers known as the
Servants of India. But there came into Jagadisanji's life
the tragedy of leprosy. It was while he was thus afflicted
that he met Dr. Robert Cochrane. The story of their
meeting is a remarkable one. It is not, I believe, a tale
of pure chance, but of God using unexpected means to
bring a man of compassion into touch with another man
for whom He had a great work to do, and who was eager
to serve but who saw nothing but frustration and loneliness facing him. Dr. Cochrane was asked to give a review
over All India Radio of a book by Perry Burgess, *Who
Walk Alone*. The book is now so well known that I need
not refer to it in detail. The author, himself the secretary
of the Leonard Wood Leprosy Foundation, an American
organization, movingly tells the story of a U.S.A. citizen
who, contracting leprosy, comes to know the mental
agony of all those who, through no fault of their own,
" walk alone ". Now in India, where radio sets are
expensive and the people mostly poor, loudspeakers are
sometimes set up in public places, and one was set up
in Cuddalore on an open *maidan,* or park, so that all
who took the air there might have free entertainment.
Disconsolate and alone, Jagadisanji was crossing this
maidan as Dr. Cochrane's voice came over the air. At

once his attention was arrested. Was it not his own spiritual situation of despair which was being described? But the speaker did not end there; he ended with the message of the book, that these were men who should not be compelled to walk alone, that they were brothers, that they should be accorded wise friendship, helped in their need. There was something in the speaker's voice, his sincerity and earnestness, which filled him with hope. He got in touch with Dr. Cochrane, who not only treated him as a patient, but loved him as a friend, and counselled him as an older man. He saw Jagadisan's unusual qualities of mind, and the yearning longings of his heart for a noble India. He put those qualities to work on behalf of other leprosy sufferers, making him a colleague in the developing work in the Madras State of what is now the Hind Kusht Nivaran Sangh (The India Anti-Leprosy Association), and which was then the Madras branch of the India Council of the British Empire Leprosy Relief Association, about the formation of which I have written earlier in this chapter. Professor Jagadisan in time became organizing secretary; and in particular prosecuted intensive work in the Arcot Division of Madras. When Dr. Cochrane and Professor Jagadisan first met, Dr. Cochrane at once urged on Jagadisanji the enormous importance of exercising his fingers, which tended to get more cramped; and while to some extent there are still neural disabilities he is well again, and fired with the energy of a great enthusiasm; and it is a sign of the now enlightened attitude of at any rate the intelligentsia of Madras that he is an accepted and honoured social worker. In his sturdy motor, which is equipped as a dispensary, office, sleeping-quarters, kitchen, and general pick-me-up for wayfarers in need of a lift,

Jagadisanji took my wife and me on a tour of some of the national-sponsored pieces of work which he has been largely instrumental in establishing, and which are carrying on and extending and forwarding pioneer efforts of foreign missionaries. We visited out-patient clinics, centres for village visiting and survey, and a charming and simple residential Leprosy Home built in memory of the devoted wife of Mahatma Gandhi. In all of these very active centres there was a marked quality of personal concern shown for the patients; the staffs, doubtless hand-picked men, were able and enthusiastic. Here was the new India at its best, facing the sorrows and problems of its people with outstretched, serving hands. Here compassion drove out all superior condescension; here the bonds of brotherhood replaced the dividing walls of caste. Here new hope was being brought to some thousands of the many thousands of sufferers in the Madras State.

As we were taken around, charts and maps and statistics and records were expounded to us by the local doctors in charge; I am afraid I do not remember a single significant figure. But what is most significant is that they were there at all. Even twenty years ago— should I say fifteen?—it would have been unthinkable. One of the clinics was in memory of " Thakkar Baba "— Sri A. V. Thakkar—another of the Servants of India, and one who always had a special concern for leprosy sufferers. A Hindu and a poor man he had always with great regularity sent me his subscription for The Mission to Lepers, an avowedly Christian work, while I worked in India. And with it there always came a word of encouragement. He was a man of true compassion. Another clinic, about to be opened, was to be named after Father Damien, and already a large picture of him had been produced from somewhere. And, as I have just written, the Leprosy Home where we were entertained at the village of Mazhavanthangal was the Kasturba Gandhi Memorial, contributed to by admirers of that faithful, stalwart partner of Mahatma Gandhi, a husband who must so often have tried her wifely patience! As I stood there I had memories of her, nearly thirty years earlier, coming into the working room of Mahatmaji at Sabarmati, on the banks of the river, and with quiet grace serving him with a mid-morning honey and lemon drink, in which I was asked to share. Where she could not understand his ways she followed in trust; with him she was ready to suffer, even unto prison; and as she grew older she came more completely to understand him in his great endeavour. It was largely through the joint effort of Dr. Cochrane and Professor Jagadisan that Mahatma Gandhi agreed that a part of the Memorial Fund for his wife should be used for this happy, active Leprosy Home. When, six weeks before this visit to the Memorial Home, I had been the guest in New Delhi at her son Devadas's flat, I had noticed the splendid portrait of her on the walls of his simply-furnished room, showing so clearly the deep seriousness and strength of her character. As her portrait, and those of Mahatmaji, and Mrs. Devadas Gandhi's father, Sri Rajagopalachari, looked down on us, I rejoiced that Devadasji is himself deeply concerned to forward a movement to bring healing to leprosy sufferers, as a trustee of the Gandhi Memorial Leprosy Foundation.

Does this seem a diversion? I think it is not. It is all very relevant indeed to the theme I am pursuing. It has its vital relationship to a man full of leprosy crying out to a Man on the Galilean road, and His response.

VII

It is only possible to refer to one other enterprise before I pass on from this Arch of Physical Healing in the Bridge of Compassion. On the other side of Vellore from the " Place of New Life ", eight miles out and on rising, stony ground, stands the new Schieffelin Leprosy Research Sanatorium which The Mission to Lepers and in particular its grown-up daughter society American Leprosy Missions have recently provided. It is built on the lower slopes of what is called Elephant Hill, an appropriate name, for the outline of the hill is for all the world like the back of a great elephant, the outstretched trunk, the high forehead, the descending sweep of the back.

In February of 1948 I had walked over a stony stretch of deserted land, with colleagues who carried with them blueprints and measuring tapes. There were white clouds above us, like little balls of cotton-wool, moving across the cerulean blue sky. The heat of the sun struck back at us from the hard rocks. There was a range of hills on the horizon which was strikingly beautiful, but the site itself was uninviting. It was, however, all that could be found after a long search. The better, cultivable land was already fully occupied by peasants, and unprocurable. There was one natural pool, with toddy palms around it, which had caught the water from the higher slopes, but otherwise all was dry and brown. We set to work to measure the distance between significant points. We decided that, in general, the research and medical block should be here, the men's cottages there, the staff quarters a little way up the hillside, and so on. Then we thirstily got into a car again, drove away, and the site was left empty, save for the lizards basking on the stones, and an occasional bird fluttering over the prickly shrubs and near-white long grasses.

It was some time before that empty site began to take on a changed appearance. There were delays caused by changes in design and efforts to bring down the costs. There were tenders to call for, and a builder to appoint. But on September 6th, 1952, Dr. Ida Scudder, the founder of what is now the Vellore Christian Medical College, was invited by The Mission to Lepers to cut the first sod. Three months later, six commemorative stones were laid in the research and administrative building by friends invited to represent different interests —a leprosy patient from the " Place of New Life "; the pastor of the local Church in Vellore; a citizen of North Arcot; the Director of the Vellore Christian Medical College, Dr. Hilda Lazarus; a representative of the many donors in the U.S.A. of American Leprosy Missions; and another of those in many lands of The Mission to Lepers.

Mr. William Bailey, the Mission's Secretary for India, together with Mrs. Bailey, took up his residence at the earliest opportunity in a barely completed room, kept an eye on progress, and made the hundred-and-one decisions required over points of detail; and in July, 1953, Dr. Herbert Gass, the Mission's honorary medical adviser, and the professor of dermatology at Vellore Christian Medical College, and Mrs. Gass took up their residence in the medical superintendent's house. The bare site had begun to take on life.

Although buildings were by no means complete, and it was not yet possible to admit the first patients, it was very kindly arranged that while my wife and I were visiting in December, 1953, the main buildings should be dedicated to the service of God.

Why have they gone up at this time and at this rather remote site? They have gone up because it was seen that a combination of circumstances and opportunities demanded action on the Mission's part. The Mission to Lepers has in India, Burma, and Pakistan alone twenty-nine Homes, and substantially aids sixteen others. But none of them is equipped for substantial research, and none of them is in proximity to a Christian Medical College, though the Mission's Home at Miraj is near to the Medical School there, which has now changed its character and become a centre for post-graduate studies. With the ambitious plan carried out at Vellore to change a Women's Medical School into a Christian Medical College for both men and women, there came a challenge to The Mission to Lepers and to American Leprosy Missions to have nearby a residential centre where, for one thing, the students might come and train in leprosy and see a piece of Christian leprosy work in action; and where, for another, research might be engaged in. Some aspects of research must remain outside the scope and competence of the Mission; but others come within its range of possible action. Here at Karigiri, Elephant Hill, there is the development of Dr. Brand's orthopædic work to engage in; there is the whole psychological approach to the problem—both to patient and to public; there are particular studies in the pathology of the disease which Dr. Gass is well fitted to undertake; there is the comparison to be pursued as between different types of treatment. And there are still unresolved problems with regard to the transmission of the disease, which can best be studied in an endemic, rural area. We need to remember that Christ's command to His disciples to " cleanse the lepers " has immense implications—including the mental discipline of devoted, intelligent study, wedded to the spiritual discipline of understanding love.

So it was that at the service of dedication at which I was asked to speak I drew my theme from the Elephant Hill which looked down upon the gathered company. I remembered a word about bridges which I had heard the then Secretary of State for India, Mr. L. S. Amery, speak to a recently appointed Viceroy of India, Lord Wavell, and the reply which he made. Mr. Amery had counselled the Viceroy-designate to have the wisdom and caution of the Indian elephant, which always felt the strength of a bridge before it attempted to cross it. When Lord Wavell got up to reply, he said he had noted the Secretary of State's cautionary warning, and then he flashed, " But this elephant "—pointing to himself—" has got to *make* bridges." And so I urged that on Elephant Hill the workers must make bridges. I suggested that there were in particular three tasks of bridge-building to be engaged in—the establishment of a bridge between teaching and service, another between scientific knowledge and human insights, and another between the succour of temporal needs and the satisfaction of immortal longings. Here was a task ranging far beyond the merely physical; but in that, of course, is the heart of the whole matter. The physical is important and constitutes an arch in the total bridge; it is an arch which must be well built; for it is the denial of a religion of incarnation to despise the physical. But this single arch is incomplete by itself, and we must now move on to the next one, the Arch of Human Fellowship, and after that to a third one, the Arch of Eternal Hope.

THE ARCH OF HUMAN FELLOWSHIP

I

It is a truism, but one that still needs to be emphasized, that man only finds the fulfilment of his personality in community. Alone, he is insecure, baffled, frustrated. He is unable to fulfil his part in meeting others' needs, and his own need of the help of others is unmet. Health of body, mind and spirit is only found in the fulfilment of the obligations of citizenship as well as in the enjoyment of its privileges. It is one of the abiding perils of prosperity that a man in his affluence and power may imagine himself self-sufficient, and live without either fear of God, or a sense of obligation to others. But adversity soon breaks down this tragic pride. It makes him aware of his need of the help of others. And when that help is not forthcoming his isolation is desperate. Man's ultimate extremity is to be utterly alone.

Down the long years of history perhaps there are no people who have known this frustration of aloneness so much as those suffering from leprosy. It should not be so; but thus it has been. And thus, in far too many lives, it is today. It is easy to over-dramatize and exaggerate; but it is even easier, on the ground that one is not going to be swept away by false sentiment, to underrate the tribulations of others. It is a defence mechanism of selfishness to be cynical. It is far better to open one's heart in generous love, even though that inevitably exposes it to the call of others' need.

It has been the loneliness of sufferers from leprosy, even

more than their physical need, which has evoked the active compassion of the generous-hearted. The initial act of Christ in putting out His hand in friendly gesture to touch the man full of leprosy, before ever He spoke the healing word, displayed His complete insight into the man's deepest craving. Was it not also thus with the Knights of St. Lazarus, that early Christian Order for the service of victims of leprosy, in which the Knights utterly identified themselves with their patients by sharing with them a common life? Or with St. Francis, as he lifted the mutilated hand of the beggar whom a few minutes before he had turned away from in contempt, and kissed it? So one might continue to give early Christian examples of this outgoing friendship, this mighty simplicity of action quickened by love. This was the dynamic energy which created whatever constructive effort was engaged in during medieval times to bring back the isolated leprosy sufferer from " without the camp " into the community of human fellowship.

It is not surprising, therefore, that within the modern missionary movement one may find again and again those who have engaged in pioneer leprosy work not primarily as doctors, or as preservers of public health, but in sheer friendship, and with a desire to transform lonely men into co-operating members of society.

In the recent tour which my wife and I made in India and farther East I had frequent opportunities of seeing at particular places what friendship had achieved. And I will therefore illustrate the generalizations I have made by describing one or two of the many centres of community life which we visited, made up of men and women and children who had severally experienced this cold shadow of aloneness.

There was, for instance, our visit to Champa. On either side of the railway track the rice harvest was ripening from goldy-green to pale biscuit as our train neared this wayside station on a morning in late November, 1953. Lavender blue hills showed pale on the northern horizon, only the slightest shade different from the sky above them. Doubtless the country looked much the same fifty-three years before when P. A. Penner, the first missionary from the U.S.A. to be sent out to India by the General Conference Mennonite Mission, alighted at the same one-platform halt. It must have been a strange feeling for this pioneer, without the people's language, without friends to meet him, and without a house to go to, to be set down with his luggage in the very heart of rural India, in an area entirely unevangelized, and just begin his work from *there*. Save that he knew God was with him, he was alone. But for us, all was so different. Our host, Mr. Jantzen, was there to meet us; other friends to carry our luggage; a motor car to take us by a dusty track past the mission general hospital and its staff houses to the bungalow which P. A. Penner had in time built and where I had so often stayed with him. And then there was coffee to refresh us on arrival.

I have told before* the story of how, while Penner was still living in a temporary hut, a couple of men came to him begging, because they were disfigured " lepers ", and no one wanted them. And he, who prayed every day for God's guidance, saw them as men wanting friendship, and not simply the alms of a few copper coins. His mid-day meal was cooking, and he made them guests, spread-

* See *Red Earth and Summer Lilies,* by A. Donald Miller. Published by the Lutterworth Press. Price 6s. 6d. in the British Isles.

The first pioneer patients land on the empty island in July, 1951. See pages 93–108

THE ISLE OF HAPPY HEALING, HONG KONG

The first building completed by the landing beach six months later, seen from the staff quarters

The Opening of the Maxwell Memorial
Medical Centre, January, 1954.
See pages 105–107.

THE ISLE OF HAPPY HEALING
HONG KONG

Young patients outside The Lord Will's
Church, built in 1952, with their leaders.
See pages 129–130

ing before them his rice and curry. Though he could never have suspected it, he was in that act entering upon his life work, putting in the first stone of the arch of fellowship which his compassion urged him to build. *" For I was an hungred, and ye gave me meat: I was thirsty, and ye gave me drink."*

On this visit I was shown extracts from P. A. Penner's day-book, made available after his death in 1949. From it I found that it was on April 27th, 1902, that these two suppliants came. " Two lepers were fed and they were promised that we would care for them." It was in September of the same year that the next outstanding step was taken. " Sep. 13th, 1902. Zemindar gave land for the lepers. We will build them a few simple huts just as soon as possible." In a few days temporary matting shacks were erected on a site near the river, where a tree stands today marking the spot. Five days later the five first occupants were in residence, and when some clothing was given, " it was very encouraging to notice that the most degraded of the lepers was the first to say thank you for his clothes ". *" I was a stranger, and ye took me in: naked, and ye clothed me."*

So the simple diary proceeds. Other arrivals. The dilemma created by the death of a patient, and no one ready to do the burying. The beginnings of a more permanent building. The separation of the first two healthy children from leprous parents, and the appointment of a peasant woman, Pataitin, to care for them. (We met her, still alive, and a splendid Christian woman, a convert some seven years after this appointment.) Almost empty coffers and rice-bins, but on Feb. 9th, 1903, " Received $66 from a friend in Dakota today for the lepers—our leper treasury was almost empty—we had been praying for help and the dear Lord sent this just at the right time —All thanks to Him."

There were many discouragements, quarrelling among the patients and falsehoods told. There is this entry for Aug. 4th, 1903 : " There is much sin and trouble in the leper compound. One of our most faithful lepers has been involved in a shady case. May we not be discouraged, dear Lord, but strengthen us so that we may carry on Thy work unafraid." *" I was sick, and ye visited me: I was in prison, and ye came unto me."*

And then, in the middle of November, 1903, just fifty years before our own visit, the great visitor came, Thomas A. Bailey, brother of Wellesley Bailey, The Mission to Lepers' founder. It is noted that he " took some pictures " of the work, expressed his satisfaction with it, saw the need of proper buildings and then, on Nov. 19, 1903, " Mr. Bailey left today with a promise that the Mission would send £300 for building purposes. Thank you, dear God."

The yearnings and actions of compassion, so hardly tested, had now been honoured. And so began the large Home of The Mission to Lepers, today a community of over 500 people.

When we visited it on this occasion, four " Welcome " archways had been prepared. Near the entrance was one upon which were emblazoned the words " Gate of Service ". At another part of this garden village was one called " Gate of Hope "; and the two others were called " Gate of Joy " and " Gate of Healing ". They spoke of realities which were abundantly apparent in that Leprosy Home and Hospital, which itself bears the name Bethesda. Here was fellowship, an arch made up of very broken stones, but strong and joyous.

How good it was to visit the various activities of this cheerful community, to meet old friends among the patients whom I had known ten, twenty, even thirty years ago. When a welcome meeting was held in the large church building, our necks became wetter and wetter with the well-doused flower garlands with which group after group invested us. And since scent had been sprinkled in generous measure on the blooms of marigold and hibiscus and the rest, we became almost dazed with the heavy odour. There was the happy murmur of people " having a good time ", smiles without ration, hymns sung with gusto, an eager quiet while speeches were made. Again and again the note of gratitude was struck in the various welcome addresses, gratitude to the unseen friends in far-away lands and towns and villages who had brought this contented company out of loneliness into fellowship. What did a few missing fingers matter? Or lameness? Or the loss of physical beauty of feature? Or even blindness? Now they were a people who " belonged ".

We saw something of the many activities of this well-ordered, well-kept village. There was the weaving of gaily-coloured cloth, for shirts or saris or other purposes. There was a group of old patients, simple peasant folk, hammering at rock to make small stones for road-making. Out in the sunshine they chattered and sang happily together with the click, click, click of their hammers sounding as a regular background. It was surprising to see the resourcefulness shown by those who hadn't complete hands, in order that they could wield a hammer. Then there were others tending flower and vegetable gardens. Farmwork is not yet extensive, for lack of adequate suitable land, but waste land was being levelled and improved for future cultivation. A few of the more intelligent patients were employed in the dispensary, and others had been trained in simple nursing in the over-full hospital wards. We discussed with the American doctor and nurse the enlargement of the medical block as a " Penner Memorial ", and also other building projects. And then we visited the children's school. The Champa Home is placing special emphasis on the care of children who have leprosy in its more severe, or lepromatous, form. On the classroom walls pictures of national leaders abounded, with a fine impartiality of political allegiance! There was also a photograph of the little Lancashire lady whose gift to celebrate her seventieth birthday and thank God for the many blessings He had showered on her had made possible the first of the school buildings. Friendliness was of the essence of her own vivacious character, as I can testify; and the memory of Mrs. Kirkham is sweet to many.

We moved to the scrupulously clean compound where the girls of the Home lived, the Spencer Jack Memorial. My mind flashed back to a Sunday night in 1949, windy and cold, at Invercargill in New Zealand, the most southerly city in the world. In my travels I had reached right down there, for there are friends of the Mission in that far outpost, and they too wanted to hear directly of the work. The church had, I remember, an illuminated cross over its tower, shining there in the night away towards the South Pole. The service over, I went down to the porch, where an icy wind was blowing, to bid goodnight to friends. A small lady, very simply dressed, whispered up at me, " I'm Spencer Jack's mother," and I was glad that I at once recalled the name. For Spencer Jack's mother was a lady who turned a deep personal sorrow into a great occasion to bring others joy. She was a poor widow, and her one son Spencer wanted to be a medical missionary. In particular he wanted to befriend those in need because of leprosy. While he was at school she skimped and saved for his medical education; and then, while he was still a medical student, he died. Instead of being resentful she gave the money which she had saved for his medical education to the work to which he had dedicated himself; and then went on, by austere living, to add to that gift. That was the beginning of the girl's compound at the Champa Home which now I was visiting again. The southern tip of New Zealand and the heart of India were brought together there by the act of a Christian woman who wanted to bring fuller life to children who were not her own, but whom she loved as she had loved her own son Spencer. And here, because of a transmuted sorrow turned into saving deed, had been established a work which was bringing new life and laughter to some of India's neediest children.

When I spoke to the patients at the welcome meeting my interpreter was a tall young man, who now holds a staff job at the Home and who as a boy was a patient. At the Home he was educated; there, too, after long treatment, he found healing of body; and there, too, he came to faith in Christ as his Saviour. In his spare time from work he was reading as an external student for his Arts degree. He translated readily and easily for me into the local Chhattisgarhi dialect of Hindi; and it was grand to feel as we stood side by side that we were both there because of the friendship of Christian people in many lands. This young man was but one of a long succession of young people, whether at the Home at Champa or at other Homes, who have demonstrated the constructive, saving consequences of practical acts of fellowship. It cannot be too strongly contended at a time when the distracted state of the world leads some to lift their eyes longingly to far horizons for the vindication by God of His regnancy, that the emphasis of Christ's own teaching in the Gospel story was repeatedly on compassionate neighbourliness towards the immediate man in need and not on the far-away look. Preparedness for the future was achieved by attention to the needs of the here and now. The story of the Good Samaritan contains profound theology as well as a moving humanism. The outcast Samaritan who went out of his way to help the half-dead man beaten up by robbers did not only bind up his wounds and put him on his own beast. By doing that out of a loving heart, with no calculating ulterior motive, he unconsciously put himself in the line of inheritance of eternal life. In answer to His questioner's poser as to how he might inherit eternal life, Jesus was declaring in this story the inseparable if invisible bond between yearning for eternal salvation and acts of simple human friendship.

II

It was just before I had visited Champa that I saw at Lucknow in North India a most arresting demonstration of the part which service of leprosy sufferers has in the building of the arch of fellowship. The Mission to Lepers has never been a Society addicted to conferences. I think it can be said that the extensive business of its Council is done with the minimum of disturbance of people's time and movements, and also of typing, paper, and office elaboration. Moreover, the increasingly scattered centres of work, and the widely separated distances between groups of contributors, make gatherings for conference impossible on a large scale. But it did seem well to the Mission's Council that, after nearly eighty years of service without an international gathering, the time had come for a limited number of delegates from many lands to meet in conference, both to strengthen a sense of unity, and to discuss in prolonged working sessions matters of common concern for the furtherance of this task of the Kingdom of God.

An admirable account of this Conference has already been written by my colleague, Wilfred Russell, in his *Life More Abundant*,* which was the theme-title of the Conference; and it is not my purpose faintly to echo what has been already said so clearly and so well. All I want to do is to share with the reader one or two of the overwhelming impressions which the Conference made on me in relation to the vital matter of fellowship. Of the notable contributions of medical delegates, including such renowned leprologists as Dr. Muir, Dr. Cochrane, Dr. Gass, Dr. Brand, Dr. Davey (thirty-four of the delegates were doctors among a total of seventy-two; and apart from participating visitors) I must not write, or I would be drifting back again to the subject of the last chapter. Suffice it to say that their united statement and recommendations at the end of the Conference were of real importance, and of much value in providing a blueprint for the best future direction of the Mission's medical effort.

The first impression was at the Roll Call of the Conference. During Friday and Saturday delegates had been arriving from north, east, south and west. The India

* *Life More Abundant,* by Wilfred H. Russell. Published by The Mission to Lepers. Now out of print.

delegates entertained us first of all in the hotel garden to tea, when the shrill shriek of hundreds of green parakeets, who were having a final chatter in the trees before going to sleep, competed with our own informal conversations. Then we went to the conference hall as darkness fell. There should have been multitudes of tiny lights outlining the buildings of the city against the night sky, for it was the time of *Dewali,* the Hindu festival of lights. But there had been a university students' riot and there was a curfew order in force which spoilt the festival. Moreover, the street-lighting system in our part of Lucknow had been put out of action by the rioters. Indeed, a small platoon of soldiers kept watch outside the hotel garden during the night.

But if there was darkness and division outside, there was light and fellowship within. When the Roll Call was taken, it revealed that there were delegates present from thirteen States of India (and it must be remembered that India is almost a sub-continent, with many languages), Japan, Thailand, Hong Kong, Burma, Pakistan, Uganda, the Union of South Africa, Belgian Congo, Portuguese Cameroons, Nigeria, Greece, Switzerland, Denmark, Great Britain, Ireland, the U.S.A., Canada, Australia, New Zealand. We were a truly international group. Denominationally, there were Anglicans, Lutherans, Baptists, Methodists, members of the Church of India, Burma, Pakistan and Ceylon, Church of South India, Church of Ireland, Reformed and Evangelical Church, Church of the Brethren, " Plymouth " Brethren, Society of Friends, Swiss Reformed Church, Syrian, Presbyterian, Congregational, Greek Orthodox, Mennonite, United Church of Canada, and a Japanese Church the name of which I do not know. I may have left one or two others out. But that does not matter. At Lucknow we were all one, both in a single, particular service of the Lord Jesus, and because He had welcomed us into His embrace despite all our frailties. Here was fellowship. And it was a fellowship which issued from compassion. Some of the representatives had spent year after year pleading on behalf of those inarticulate thousands with leprosy who needed help, in order that funds might be available for their succour. Their fellowship was expressed in journeys on wet nights, small audiences, the strain of constant preaching and speaking. Others were doctors who had forsaken the glittering prizes of professional careers to stand in with folk who looked to them in their naked need, serving them without thought of reward. Others were nurses who knew the grind and wear, in baking or steaming climates, of all the detail work of carrying through small hospital routines; the anxieties of working with helpers only partially trained and often partly disabled; the tasks repellent, often so repellent, in themselves. The fellowship of these doctors and nurses was in the dedication of their skills and their sympathies to those accounted least. Others were administrators, " serving tables ", seeing to the fabric of organization that there should be no rent in it, engaged in background work, unseen but essential. Others represented Council, those men and women who, chosen for their Christian wisdom and experience and enthusiasm, gladly give of these qualities for the right direction and prosecution of the work. Others represented the great company of voluntary helpers, contributors, representatives in far-away villages or towns or cities. The fellowship of these was in their unwavering faithfulness and generosity and concern. Truly the little group in Dublin seventy-nine years before which brought The Mission to Lepers into being were doing something which has achieved more than ever they could have dreamed.

It was very fitting that the oldest member of the Conference, Dr. Neville Bradley, should lead our family prayers that first night. He and Mrs. Bradley, who was also with us, had engaged in missionary leprosy work as far back as 1905 when they laboured at Pakhoi in China. Now Dr. Bradley is a valued member of Council. And it was equally appropriate that, beautifully and very simply leading our thoughts, he should remind us that the arch of fellowship in which we were rejoicing had its keystone at Calvary, " the greatest meeting-place of all ". He depicted what Christ had done, even as He hung upon the Cross, to bring hope and comfort and love to the centurion, to the penitent thief, and to His Mother and the disciple John. Even in that scene of utter brokenness, and willingly accepted loneliness, Christ was the bringer of healing fellowship. The meeting-place of all men was in Him.

It was at this deepest level that our fellowship was made evident the following morning, when we made our way to Christ Church for participation in the central act of Christian worship. There ought not to be anything at all remarkable when Christians of various denominations and nationalities unite in making a corporate act of thanksgiving to God for the redeeming sacrifice of Calvary, made for each one of them and accepted by them all. Nor that they should at that act together make their communion, as side by side they receive the symbols of bread and wine. " This do in remembrance of Me." It is terrible that it should be remarkable. But so it is. There, in the sunlit church where we met, we were all one. The Bishop of Lucknow had warmly invited us, and he led the celebration himself. Anglican and Mennonite, Greek Orthodox and Brethren, Presbyterian and Quaker, we were first of all redeemed brethren in Christ, and servants of His Kingdom. On our knees in prayer, and coming to our Lord for the Bread of His own Life, we met in our common need and in our common faith. Surely it is at the place where we remember in penitence and yet in gladness the supreme reconciling act of God that Christians must find again their own lost unity. There is, fundamentally, only One Communion, as there is only One Lord, One Faith, One Baptism. And can it be that so long as Christians divide at this central act of thanksgiving, fellowship and Divine refreshment they dare hope for a larger unity? Thank God that at Lucknow we were a company of delegates, both at the Anglican Church on the first Sunday, and at the Methodist Episcopal Church on the second Sunday, which was wholly united. As I worshipped I could not but reflect upon the strange and stirring fact that it was the loneliness of the man suffering from leprosy, and our common endeavour to bring to him fellowship in Christ's name, which had brought us to this complete identification of ourselves with one another. Whatever be the mystery of physical suffering—and deep in hidden shadow does much of it lie—this surely is abundantly clear, that somehow both the offering of suffering and the service of suffering are instruments of reconciliation, whether divine or human.

III

An act of fellowship of another kind was engaged in the next day, when the formal opening of the Conference took place at an historic Lucknow building, the Chhattar Manzil Palace, now adapted for the purposes of the Government of India Central Drug Research Institute.

When the matter of the proposed Conference was brought before His Excellency Sri K. M. Munshi, the Governor of Uttar Pradesh (the United Provinces of the old days), he showed a most friendly desire to offer hospitality to the delegates and goodwill towards the work. Not only was he ready to preside at the formal opening session, but he entertained the delegates later in the week to a garden party in the beautifully maintained grounds of Government House, a band playing for the pleasure of the company; and in other ways demonstrated his sympathy. To attend this opening session the Health Minister, Government of India, made a special flight from Delhi early in the morning. She is a very noble woman in the life of India, Rajkumari Amrit Kaur. Of brilliant mind and with a deep patriotism which cares intensely for the individual citizen in his particular need, she was both the first woman and the first Christian to hold a place in the Cabinet of the Prime Minister, Sri Jawaharlal Nehru. For many years before national independence came to India in August, 1947, she had been a very close lieutenant of Mahatma Gandhi, sharing the austerities and the hazards of close association with that redoubtable leader. And so we had on the platform the Hindu Governor of the Province, and the Christian Health Minister for India. Beside them was the Bishop of Lucknow to lead our prayers. And among the distinguished audience which had come to show their goodwill were Sikhs and Muslims. Sardar Bahadur Balwant Singh Puri, handsome and immaculate, the Sikh general secretary of the India Red Cross Society and of the Hind Kusht Nivaran Sangh, also flew over specially from Delhi, another act of goodwill added to very many in the past which he had engaged in to help on the Mission's work. Government officials, social workers, doctors, research chemists, university professors, all were there, together with the delegates of the Conference. The occasion both expressed fellowship and became an instrument of stronger fellowship. One could but rejoice that in this service of suffering we all had so much to bring us together. I have always failed to understand the hesitancy of some Christians to share with non-Christians on a level of mutual esteem in the practical, immediate service of men's needs. For there is reason for rejoicing in this, and a God-given opportunity for strengthening the bonds of brotherhood. The Gospels very pointedly describe the absolutely level, impartial, judgment of our Lord Jesus Christ in relation to a man's actions of good or evil. Goodness was goodness, by whomsoever displayed. And so was evil. It was the uncovenanted Samaritan who won our Lord's commendation when a fallen man by the wayside needed help, for it was he who " had compassion on him ". It was a Samaritan who was the only one among ten who returned to give thanks for healing from leprosy, and Christ was quick to appreciate that graciousness. And there was the occasion when the disciples in hot, but mistaken, loyalty were indignant at one who did not belong to their own company, but yet in Christ's name cast out devils. They forbade him, " because he followeth not with us ". But Christ was more generous in His ample love. " Forbid him not: for he that is not against you is for you." It is a sad occasion, and grievous to the loving heart of our Lord, when an absolutely sincere recognition and welcome are not given to every act of generous humanity. The service of human need, by whomsoever engaged in, helps build the arch of fellowship, so essential a part of the Bridge of Compassion.

It was humbling to hear the generous words spoken by our distinguished Chairman, and then by the special speaker. In his remarks, H.E. Sri K. M. Munshi, the *Rajyapal,* or Governor, contrasted the difference which had taken place when mercy and science combined to change the miserable condition of sufferers from leprosy in India. He recalled that it was through a missionary who had begun his life in India in the very State in which we were met that the vital change had begun. " Work in this direction (to mitigate the plight of advanced victims of leprosy) began with Mr. Bailey, who founded The Mission to Lepers, and the call came to him to missionary endeavour in Faizabad." He contrasted this work of friendship, which brought life and hope, with the tragic lot of a man with leprosy who wrote to Sir John Lawrence, the ruler of the Punjab a little over a century ago, and so moved his heart that he issued the fiat : " Thou shalt not burn thy widows; thou shalt not kill thy daughters; thou shalt not bury alive thy lepers."

This was the letter Sir John Lawrence had received : " I am weary of life; I wish to die; my life is a plague and disgust to the whole village, and my death is earnestly longed for. It is well known to all that for a leper to consent to die, to permit himself to be buried alive, is approved by the gods. I therefore solicit your permission

to be buried alive. The whole village wishes it, and I am
happy and content to die."

The Chairman was followed by a full and important
statement by the Health Minister, who stood before us in
her simple homespun sari, frail in appearance, but mighty
in her manifold activities. A note of friendship was struck
at once in her generous appreciation of what others were
doing.

" Nothing gives me greater pleasure than to be associated with a band of people who continuously preach the
gospel of ' Service before Self ' and who are engaged in
the selfless and humanitarian work of rehabilitating a
despised section of the community who happen to be
afflicted by a chronic mutilating disease like leprosy."

As Health Minister, the speaker warmed our hearts by
telling of plans which State Governments were now evolv-
ing, and of other evidences of a national awakening of
conscience. She rejoiced at the co-operation between
official and non-official bodies.

"A very heartening feature in both governmental and
non-governmental endeavour in leprosy work is the spirit
of wholehearted co-operation that prevails and is exem-
plified in a concerted effort to evolve a common policy
on all fronts."

Finally, the Rajkumari spoke of the welcome which
awaited Christian servants of the needy, from whatever
land they came.

" I am sure they will always be welcome here not only
in their personal capacity, not only for the service they
render and the example they set, but also as harbingers
of international goodwill. I am sure, too, that they will
work with us to relieve distress, to banish ignorance and
to build up the India of our dreams. In such work there
can be no question of caste or creed or racial barriers,
for the human family is indeed one. That is surely the

Gospel which the Lord Jesus preached and for which He gave His life a ransom for many. Friends, I thank you once again for the opportunity you have given me to be with you during this memorable conference and to express my deep sympathy with the cause you have espoused."

Here, indeed, sturdy stones were being laid in building the arch of fellowship.

IV

It is not at all necessary to tell of the proceedings of the Conference day by day. The three scenes I have described are sufficient to illustrate what the Conference stood for in terms of bridge-building. We saw in action the cement which binds together, heals division, and creates the structure of true peace. But I would like to tell of a visit which delegates made, when the main work of the Conference was completed, after a week of spirited discussions.

We all on the final day went on pilgrimage to Faizabad, eighty miles distant, the place to which the Governor had referred in his address at the formal opening. At this country town Wellesley Bailey had decided to renounce his intention of taking a commission in the police force in order that he might become a missionary of the Gospel, and it was this decision which proved to be the first step leading on to the foundation of The Mission to Lepers. Now, a few miles out of Faizabad, there stands a Leprosy Home and Hospital of the Mission which was established seventeen years ago. And all delegates were invited to be present at the opening of a new development of this vigorous institution—the Wellesley Bailey Memorial Children's Sanatorium.

In the windless November air of early morning, the sunlight still cool and pleasant, delegates like boys let out of school climbed into motor buses, ready for a day's outing. Except for those who were long familiar with the roads of Uttar Pradesh, the experience was a captivating, if uncomfortable, one. Beside the straight roads great trees stood sheltering and sentinel. Beyond them were level fields, stretching away to the horizon. Crops of sugar cane thrust up their tough, thickly-leaved stalks. Here and there were clumps of pampas grass, crowned with feathery grey plumes. Winter seeds which had recently been sown were just piercing through the ground and creating pale green strips of carpet. Crops of lentils waited to be harvested. Between the fields were narrow divisions made by raised earth; and along them, single file, groups of peasants moved. The plumage of occasional peacocks flashed emerald and blue in the sunlight. Monkeys jumped off the branches of trees and lolloped across the road. Disdainful camels, grey-brown and heavily loaded, padded slowly by. At times we passed clusters of mud-walled cottages, set among bamboo groves. And the whole scene was drenched in golden sunshine.

But there was one feature which did not appeal to the company—the white powdery dust which rose in clouds as traffic churned it up. In at the sides of the motor buses, up from the floors, on to one's clothes, into one's eyes and mouth and nose, the dust poured. It was a less smart, and a much more thirsty, delegation which arrived at the Leprosy Home at noon than the one which had left Lucknow, all fresh and dandy, in the early morning!

It was good, for one who had stood on a waste of empty land in 1937, to see it now, so different. The development of this Home through the years has been described else-

77

where, its transformation into a place of healing, a model farm, a centre of constructive activity. What I immediately would like to touch upon is the transformation which has taken place in terms of fellowship. For at this single Home may be illustrated the change which is going on in many others.

I remember the first day of my arrival to begin to build on that stretch of land, salty and barren. When the nearest villagers heard a Leprosy Home was to be built on it they resisted strongly. Indeed, the Indian official with whom I had carried on detailed correspondence over the site wrote to me a week or two before I was due to go and begin building, asking whether I would not prefer to defer action until, he hoped, feeling had died down. I decided to carry on; but was met on my arrival at the rural house where my wife and I were to make temporary headquarters by a police sub-inspector who said, " Sir, I will arrange for a police escort to accompany you whenever you go to the site." I was alarmed at the thought of having a personal guard, seeing how fatal it would be to the creation of good feeling if the villagers saw me for the first time protected by the strong arm of the law. " Thank you very much," I said, " but please no." " Well, sir, will you have a policeman sleep with you at night?" asked the anxious officer. I hid my amusement at the way he put his offer, and gratefully declined the proposal.

It was evening when I went down to the site. A couple of blue-throated *nilkanth* birds were my only companions as I tramped around, and endeavoured to envisage in my mind's eye a little town of cottages and hospital and church. No villagers appeared, but perhaps they looked on from a distance. How should the buildings be arranged in relation to one another? And when they were up, who would be the people to turn this dead spot into life? What would be the steps, the vicissitudes, the obstacles, before this silent scene should ring with laughter and echo with songs to God's praise?

Now all was so different. The place almost literally hummed with life. Smiling, Dr. Chandy, the resident superintendent and medical officer, greeted us, as did the members of the staff. The patients did not wait in stiff official rows, but as we moved around the Home greeted us with warm, if sometimes shy, eagerness. This was *their* Home, in which they could take pride as they showed us their crops, their gardens, their schools, their hospital, their church. Here was fellowship, the happy company which had grown from the one lonely man who, weeks before the first buildings were ready, had limped up to me and asked if, even if he could not yet be taken in, he might shelter under the verandah of a cottage, completed up to roof level, and somehow fend for himself. " If I leave I have nowhere to go; and if I stay you will take me in when you can."

It was not given to me to do more than build during the first year the original cottages, staff quarters, and hospital, and to welcome the first patients who came during the two brief months I continued to be there after the Home was opened to patients. Its main development was carried through by colleagues, and especially by Dr. Chandy, who has been there since the day when, on August 1st, 1938, the first seven waiting men were admitted. When I left, my colleague, the Rev. W. H. Russell, became the honorary superintendent for a time, but before I quote from a story he told me I would like to give one very early illustration of the quick springing-up of the spirit of responsible citizenship among the first twenty patients whom I received in the first few days. It so happened that immediately after the Home was opened for service the whole district suffered torrential and continuous rain for several days, and hundreds of square miles were flooded. Thousands of villagers became temporarily homeless just at the time when these chronic homeless ones had found shelter and protection. So in the second week, when I was issuing to the men their ration of uncooked rice and flour for the next seven days, I said to them, " You see that earthen pot I have put on the edge of the verandah. It is empty, and I have put it there because of all the flood victims who have been driven from home just when you have found one yourselves. If you would like to help the Flood Relief Fund by putting a handful or so of your ration in the pot, I will see that its value is sent forward. I thought you might like to help." I said no more, but it was enough; and it was with joy that I watched these men give variously from their pittance of rice or wheat. It was the first step from isolation to community, from dependence on others to the service of them. It straightened their backs, and strengthened their wills.

Later, not very long after I had left, Mr. Russell told me of how one day Dr. Chandy received word from a wayfarer that " there is one of your lepers a couple of miles down the road dying by the roadside." He knew none of his patients was missing, none dying. But there must be *somebody*, perhaps one who had travelled many miles to reach this new Home, and who had fallen exhausted by the way. And so it proved to be. He said to four patients whom he was training to be ward assistants in the hospital block, " Take the stretcher and bring this brother in." One of the bearers was a Muslim, two were Hindus, one a Christian. But all had caught the spirit of service from Chandy's own example. In time they returned with a famished and dying man. He was put in the hospital ward, given warm milk, rested, washed, tended, fed. And he did not die. A day or two later Wilfrid Russell visited him in the ward; and the attendant told him of how he had been brought in. And, said Mr. Russell, there was one comment which this weak and broken man continued to repeat, " Sahib, when they picked me up they didn't even ask my name; they didn't even ask my name." To him the miracle was that there was no enquiry made which would—by reason of his distinctive name—reveal whether he were Hindu or Muslim, high caste or low. He was just a man in need, and these became his brothers as they hastened to help him.

From such beginnings the Home advanced, a startling testimony to all around, an effective instrument of good-will. The hostile neighbouring villagers soon became friends, even before I had been there many months, and it was not many years before Dr. Chandy wrote of their active co-operation. A new additional well was needed, and : —

" The local villagers offered their help, and on the day when the foundation of the well was laid they con-tributed their offerings along with those of the patients, and in half an hour more than half the cost of the well was realized. On such occasions one hears the jubilant cry, ' *Yisu Masih ki Jai* '—Victory to Jesus Christ. There was a time when this cry was seldom heard in the villages round about Faizabad. There is now hardly any village from which a patient has not come to the Home, either as an in-patient or an out-patient, and when the patient goes back home he spreads the good tidings of a place where the lepers are cleansed, where friendliness is the rule, and where truth reigns supreme."

What a joy it was now therefore to be present at the formal opening of this new development, the Wellesley Bailey Memorial Children's Sanatorium ! True, the buildings were not all ready, but the opportunity was too good to miss for declaring the sanatorium open, and enabling the first twenty-two children with leprosy to move into their new quarters. How well we were provided for ! A piping hot meal of curry and rice to eat, and the Pipers' Band of the Faizabad Police Force to play to us. Then came the ceremony itself, and the crowds who attended—the 240 patients from the main Home, the Christian community from Faizabad, the Colonel of the regiment, senior officers of the civil government, doctors of the Faizabad Medical Association, friends from the general public, the peasants from the surrounding villages. And from so many countries of the world there were these men and women delegates, themselves friends and servants of children such as those present. It made a lovely ending to the Conference at which we had been brought so near to one another. Now, in this final act, we were brought very close to the people we served, and through them to a great host of friends whose goodwill and practical help had been evoked.

V

While it is not possible for me to give other illustrations from within India of this creative fellowship through leprosy service, I cannot resist one which has its setting at Faizabad, and which is surely notable. Among the guests at the opening ceremony of this Children's Sana-torium was a man called Ratnaswamy. It is his story I would tell. Some years ago, Dr. Chandy, whose home is far away in the south of India, took leave from his double duties as medical officer and general superinten-dent in order to visit his relations. And while he was down in Travancore he visited a Leprosy Home at Puthencruz, run by the Salvation Army, and was invited to speak to the patients. He told them of his work in North India, and of how he lacked, in that predominantly Hindu area, Christian staff workers from among the patients. After-wards a patient came to him and said he would like to volunteer for service, if Dr. Chandy would give him a chance. He was a convert to Christianity. He had leprosy in its tuberculoid, or neural, form, and his right hand was already crippled. But he had great qualities of heart, and was well educated; and it was clear to Dr. Chandy that here was a young man who should be encouraged in his desire to work and witness in a far land. So Ratnaswamy came to Faizabad as a patient, and soon he became a sweet and strong influence for good in the Home. I have beside me a letter which he wrote to the lady in England who took responsibility for his support, and who had written to him a friendly letter of good cheer. It is a letter worth quoting.

"I am grateful to you for having thought of writing a letter to me across the seas, and I thank you for your assurances that you do remember my poor self in your prayers. I am delighted to hear about your son and daughter who have given their hearts to Jesus, and your beloved partner who is doing good work among the young people as a Sunday School teacher.

"I think you will be interested to hear a few things about me. I am aged twenty-eight, and have been a victim of this disease for the last eleven years. I have been living in this hospital for the last two years and my condition is by far the better than it was before. My right hand is deformed and is a permanent casualty of this disease and so I am writing this letter to you with my left hand.

" I belong to the Salvation Army but other members of my family belong to the Roman Catholic Church. One of my two elder brothers is still a Hindu, but all the other members of our family have accepted Christ Jesus as their personal Saviour. Please pray for my brother who still remains unconverted.

" This hospital is situated in a Hindu-majority area and naturally the inmates are predominantly Hindus. There are only six Christian patients here, including myself. Apart from the Christian activities carried on by the Mission, we feel that a heavy responsibility devolves upon us also because we have to show by our example and love what a blessed state it is to be a Christian— a lover of the Lord Jesus Christ! I have not much to give to Jesus but I am doing my little bit in His Name. I am doing a little help to the ward patients—brethren less fortunate than myself—and it is a source of great satisfaction and happiness to be of a little service to others, even in this my afflicted condition.

" The Medical Superintendent of this institution is Dr. P. J. Chandy, B.A., L.C.P.S., who belongs to Travancore State in South India. He is like a father to us all. He has the spirit of the Master in him; his love for the patients and his sterling character have endeared him to all of us. He is holding aloft the torch entrusted to him, and Faizabad Hospital is indeed fortunate in having him as its head. We thank the Lord for it.

" The jungle lands lying waste all around have been turned to rich fertile fields yielding wheat, rice and sugar-cane by the labour of the patients. There is a good church building for us, and we assemble there for daily prayers, and on Sundays we have special services."

There also came to the Home, while Sri Ratnaswamy was there, another educated patient called Sri Bijai Nath Tripathi. He was the manager of a secondary school in the district, and a voluntary worker for the Congress party. During the war years when many members of the party were sent to jail, he had for four years been a political prisoner. He attended the Home first of all as an out-patient, and was opposed to entering a Christian institution. Indeed, he later told of how he was so anti-Christian that he had taken steps to eliminate Christian masters from the school of which he was manager. But finally his condition was such that he realized he ought to become an in-patient. It was then that Ratnaswamy came to be his friend. Tripathi found himself touched by Ratnaswamy's goodness, and by his devotion to Jesus Christ. Ratnaswamy offered to have Bible study with him; and together also they attended the daily prayers. The spirit of service shown by both Dr. Chandy and Ratnaswamy warmed his own patriotic desire to serve his countrymen, and he entered more and more fully and co-operatively into the activities of the Home.

Meanwhile, treatment came to benefit both Ratnaswamy and Tripathi until they became free of active symptoms. They knew how Dr. Chandy laboured to carry the benefits of treatment as far as was physically possible in the district round about; but beyond were other areas quite unprovided for. Could they not themselves be pioneers? Ratnaswamy the Christian and Tripathi the patriot, might they not start something truly indigenous? They had experienced a transforming friendship; they had benefited by modern treatment; might they not now in fellowship go out and be builders of this arch themselves? Chandy did not want to lose their help, but he saw that he must encourage them, which he did. Tripathi had good standing and influence in the Congress party, and when he and Ratnaswamy went north to Gorakhpur, where leprosy was prevalent, they were offered a building which had been used for refugees. They secured local financial support, formed a committee, began their work, and later, with the help of the Gandhi Leprosy Foundation, secured a permanent site for a small Leprosy Home. Here was a magnificent venture of faith. And the work goes on, no " mission enterprise ", but a striking consequence of it.

When I met Ratnaswamyji once more at the opening of the Children's Sanatorium, I eagerly held out my hand to shake his own. And then, as I felt it in mine, crippled and nerveless, I remembered this permanent injury of his. I looked around for Paul Brand, and when I had found him I asked him to examine the hand, which he did, and he said he could bring, by his tendon transplantation operation, some new life into those crippled fingers. Arrangements were made for Ratnaswamy to go later to Vellore, and I was delighted a few months ago to receive a letter from him.

" I was in Vellore till the end of January, and I had a very profitable time there. Apart from the joy of having a new hand with improved movements, I enjoyed thoroughly the companionship of the consecrated workers there during that period.

" Yes, my hand has improved a lot by Dr. Brand's operation. Tendon transplantation and skin grafting were done. . . . I am extremely satisfied and am grateful to God for what He has done to me.

" Our work is going on well here, and we are now putting more emphasis on the out-patient work. Apart from the out-patient work at Gorakhpur itself, we have five out-patient clinics in the neighbouring districts, all directed from the Gorakhpur centre. About a thousand patients come for treatment every week in these clinics. A maximum number of patients are benefiting by the minimum amount of expenditure. Neither have we increased the strength of the staff which will be usually needed for the maintenance of our *Ashram* which has now a strength of seventy indoor patients."

It is of much significance that this enterprise, led by a Christian and a Hindu in loving partnership, should so clearly and openly uplift and hold in high honour the name of Jesus Christ. Not only does Ratnaswamy hold Christian worship at the Home, but he was used on one occasion to bring about a reconciliation between two factious churches in the town of Gorakhpur, by inviting them both to come and take part in a united service. For this became the occasion of a restored fellowship. Moreover, Christmas is now celebrated in the neighbourhood by collections among the community for this pioneer leprosy work, for it is well recognized that it was the outstretched hand of Jesus which brought both fellowship and healing to the man with leprosy who called out to Him, and set in motion a new and constructive concern for all who are in similar need. "As usual," Ratnaswamyji wrote me only shortly before I write these lines, " we shall also be celebrating Christmas here in the *Ashram*. Baba Raghavdasji (a leading Hindu social worker) has issued an appeal to celebrate the Jayanti (birthday celebration) of Jesus in a fitting manner and to observe the Christmas week as the leprosy week. Local churches at Gorakhpur will be approached to visit the *Ashram* and address the inmates."

We must now move farther East, leaving unmentioned those many other evidences of creative friendship which my wife and I saw as we moved rapidly through other

Leprosy Homes in India, until we finally sailed across from Dhanushkodi to Ceylon, the last sight of India from the speeding ship being the summit of the *mandapam* of the great Rameshwaram Temple as it sank slowly behind the western horizon, the sun setting in a glowing apricot-hued sky. One sentence to sum up must suffice. In present-day India—itself a great potential bridge of reconciliation between East and West and with a unique rôle to play in drawing together countries and peoples of different political creeds and cultures—the service by Christian friends of individual men and women shadowed by leprosy has, I believe, a quite incalculable significance when it issues from true compassion and brings those who were before " without the camp " into the warmth and cheer of a welcoming fellowship.

VI

We now travelled on to a part of the world where division and active strife have continued to mar the lives of people and nations since World War II came to its supposed termination. To Malaya, with its guerilla jungle warfare still proceeding. To Hong Kong, whose million and more refugees from the mainland told their tale of the great revolution in living and ideas and government going on in China. To Formosa, with its island people freed from Japanese domination, now subject to the government of Nationalist China, and a trigger-point in the wider strategies of power politics. To Japan, a defeated nation, stripped of its earlier possessions and endeavouring to adapt itself to its new and humbler status. To Korea, battered and torn, the cockpit of outside forces representing opposing ideologies and ambitions, not of its own creation. And, while we did not travel to Indo-China with its prolonged internal and colonial warfare, or Burma with its inner conflicts and tensions, we realized that these countries also shared in the present shattering events and movements in the Far East which, please God, may be as the earthquake which precedes a better rebuilding from the dust.

Was it fantasy, wishful thinking, to suppose that in such a cataclysmic situation a work of practical service for the one and the one and the one in dire need because he had leprosy could have any effective part in bringing liberty to peoples and nations? Could the arch of fellowship be built here? Had compassion a more mighty power to deliver than compulsion? I am sure it was not fantasy, but faith; and while faith must often wait with long patience before it is proved to be true, yet there are other times when in the Divine goodness auguries and visible signs are quickly vouchsafed to give fresh courage.

So it was that we were privileged to see something, in these unquiet and unhappy lands, of the quiet and happy building of " the things that make for peace ". In the remainder of this chapter I shall confine my illustrations of this saving struggle in the Far East almost wholly to a new venture of The Mission to Lepers at Hong Kong, after a shorter reference to government leprosy work in Malaya; though I want to reserve a little space of illustrations from Africa. But in the next chapters, when we come to consider the effect of Christian leprosy work in building up hope in the goodness and eternal purpose of God for man, we shall move on farther to Formosa and Korea and Japan.

As we travelled to Hong Kong we called briefly at the ports of Penang and Singapore, and also visited Kuala

Lumpur. And while we sailed through the pale and placid waters of the Andaman Sea and passed the thickly-forested northern coastline of Sumatra on our starboard side, I thought of a paragraph I had read some months earlier in *The Times,* and had cut out and kept. This is what it said :—

Singapore, April 29.

"An Indonesian leper boy who had been left in a leaking sampan to drown was found off the coast of Sumatra by a freighter and brought to Penang on Friday. He is now at the Pulau Jerejak leper camp.

"The boy told the crew of the ship he had been taken from his house at Kota Raiah, Sumatra, by two strangers who carried him to the sampan, which they towed out to sea. They cast off the sinking craft about 15 miles out. Without food and water, he had bailed out the sampan for two days before being rescued."

It was a dramatic highlight which vividly pin-pointed a situation not often so extreme, but all too frequently actual in one form or other of social ostracism or neglect or cruelty. The next day I visited the very camp or settlement to which this boy was taken, and where he had found friendship and care. It is a settlement financed and staffed by government, a small island at one time reserved entirely for leprosy patients, but now also used as a quarantine station, and as a tuberculosis centre. Different bays, separated from one another by enclosing hills, have housing for the different activities of the island. The leprosy work has been maintained for many years, and I find that a secretary of The Mission to Lepers paid warm tribute to it when he paid a visit in 1908. That the British Government should as far back as that have shown so constructive a concern is testimony to that Government's character. The Mission to Lepers' part has been a small but not unimportant one, in making it possible for missionaries and Malayan and Chinese Christian pastors from Penang to pay regular visits to these cut-off people, lead worship, and give help in the organization of social life. Mr. Adams, the present missionary of the Brethren, took us out, through the clean, prosperous city of Penang, and then by a State launch, to the two bays where some 400 leprosy patients live. We were greeted by a patients' band, complete with euphonium, cornet, clarinet, and drums, playing to us the " Marseillaise " ! I have not discovered the reason for the choice of tune; but it was a good stirring air to welcome us with. What struck me, and this is the only point I want to emphasize, was the obvious evidence of real friendship between Mr. Adams and the patients; most intimately, of course, with the Christian patients who attend worship at the Gospel Hall, and where we joined them. Men brought to Mr. Adams their shopping lists, or asked him to use his good offices in some family complication on the mainland. How strongly they contrasted with that frightened and unwanted boy seized by paid agents and taken out to sea to drown or die of thirst ! Here at Pulau Jerejak was the flowering of fellowship in place of those evil weeds of fear. Here that boy might be loved back into life. One girl asked Mr. Adams to buy for her some shoes, and so with a newspaper placed on the ground he promptly marked out the shape and size of her foot. In that one act resides a wealth of significance.

And at Sungei Buloh, some fifteen miles outside Kuala Lumpur, we had a short glimpse of an outstandingly fine piece of government leprosy work. We left behind the long array of military helicopters on the airfield—witness to the needs of jungle warfare—motored through the clean streets of Kuala Lumpur, with government and railway buildings on either side designed in Saracenic style, passed the Chinese-owned shops crowded with many wares, and moved on into the country. Armoured vehicles drove by. We passed a resettlement centre, and the ruins of a destroyed village. In time we came to a large saucer-like site set within enclosing hills. Here more than 2,400 patients live, well housed in an actively-organized community. I am not one addicted to flag-waving; but I did experience an Englishman's pride that at a time of such stress and tension the British Government should be doing so first-rate a job in this remote centre.

Such work could not have been built up without outstanding personalities, most of whom were government servants possessed with the dynamic of compassionate hearts. I cannot tell of Dr. Gordon Ryrie's work in pre-war years, and then of his determination to stand by the patients when the Japanese came in, to the great detriment of his health, but to the incalculable benefit of the patients. And I can only briefly mention the present superintendent, Dr. D. Molesworth, and the matron, Miss Good. To one long familiar with leprosy work it was instantaneously impressive that Dr. Molesworth's relations with his patients should be so manifestly friendly; and the near-adoring look of some of the men testified to the affection in which he was held. " Hello, Trouble," or " Hello, Daddy," were variations of his mode of address, always so informal, so humorous, so understanding. The matron has trained patients to become nurses of a higher standard than any I have seen among patients elsewhere. With their red, green or blue shoulder-tabs according to status they took their orders, engaged in their work, kept their eyes open to see what was wanted, with enthusiasm

omen patients cut the rice harvest

OCCUPATIONS AT THE PURULIA LEPROSY HOME AND HOSPITAL

*—and men patients lay out hand-blocked bricks to dry, for further buildings.
See pages 122–125*

Three child patients at The Isle of Happy Healing, Hong Kong, happily occupied

EARLY AND LATE

Because of modern treatment and care they will never become like this beggar woman at Calcutta with advanced tuberculoid leprosy. See pages 35–37

and efficiency. Here was a magnificent fellowship of service in a land of suspicion, a major instrument in bringing the spirit of reconciliation. I would emphasize the quite enormous importance of that conception of the Christian missionary movement which embraces not only those who work within the organized agencies of churches and societies, but all those who in government or other services abroad proclaim by their lives and work and witness the Faith which is the rock on which they stand. The Church at home has a great work to do in encouraging Christian laymen to go out to government or business or academic posts abroad with the contribution of their special technical qualifications on the one part, and with the love and understanding that their Faith has quickened in them on the other. Until the missionary movement is conceived of as something far wider than the missionary society movement it must remain confined and hampered, and not nearly adequately representative of our Lord's vision of a brotherhood of all disciples witnessing unto the uttermost of the earth.

VII

It was with impatient delight and expectation that I stood on the deck of the s.s. *Corfu* as she threaded her way slowly into the channel between the island of Hong Kong and the mainland. A grey morning mist lifted patchily, revealing great steamers, or aircraft-carriers, or the blue and brown sails of junks and sampans; then, as the mist lifted further, we saw the white buildings of Victoria, tier above tier, and finally the blue-grey hills

93

behind. By the time we drew into our berth the sun had dispersed all the mist, and the scene sparkled and shone with colour.

On the quayside a little group waved to welcome us. As soon as gangways were fixed, colleagues came aboard and our baggage was taken away by them before ever porters could get to work; and then, to our astonishment, instead of passing through the slow formalities of entering a new land, our bags were placed in a sturdy motor-launch waiting on the other side of the landing-stage. We were told to follow, the engine started up, and almost before we could get our second wind we were chuffing away to the little island, nine miles away, where in the last three years such mighty things have happened—The Isle of Happy Healing.

I want the reader to share something of the background and context of this enterprise by giving him what I believe the ciné industry calls a " flashback " to scenes and incidents a few years ago which are not unrelated to this new enterprise. At the end of 1947 I went to China, and among the stations visited was Hangchow. In *Red Earth and Summer Lilies* I have already told of the Mission Leprosy Home there, on a small hillside site within the municipal boundaries; and of its chequered story, especially during the years of war between Japan and China. I also told of the project which we felt called of God to authorize and support, the establishment of a modern leprosy agricultural settlement on an ample stretch of land out in the country near a village called Zang-peh. The offer made to us in the garden of Dr. Sturton's house at Hangchow by a Christian Chinese gentleman was the creative moment. He offered to help, both in substance and personal service, in order to set this project going.

" We were all deeply moved. Could it be that what had been mooted as far back as fifteen years ago, when our then Medical Secretary in China, Dr. James L. Maxwell, visited Hangchow and saw the need for something wider, was coming to birth as that slender, quiet Chinese gentleman talked to us, without any revealed emotion, and made this magnificent offer both of sacrificial giving, and of himself?"

The Mission to Lepers' Council, knowing all the uncertainties of the situation, firmly and gladly gave cabled authority to go forward, and sanctioned substantial financial support. As might be expected, all did not go " according to plan "; but looking back one can see the urging hand of God for us to move forward while there was time, instead of timidly waiting. For very soon a large site was secured, while the warfare in the north of China between the Kuomintang Government and the Communists moved slowly and then more swiftly southwards. Only five months after the visit of Dr. Neil Fraser, Dr. Kellersberger and myself, a little company of Christians stood on the site at Zang-peh in prayer, and commended the whole project to God. Once again bare and empty land was to blossom in fellowship, as sufferers from leprosy were served in love.

When I was back in England in the summer of 1948 I had a call one day at the Mission's headquarters from Dr. Maxwell, then a member of the Mission's Council, after his return from service in China. He was white-haired and a little bent, for he was already seventy-five years old. He sat down in the one old-fashioned mahogany armchair in my room, with its shiny black cloth upholstery. We talked of the Zang-peh project, the surprisingly rapid beginnings, the problems which would quickly arise over medical staffing. And then it was that, with complete modesty and under no sort of emotional strain, Dr. Maxwell said that, if they could be of any use, he and Mrs. Maxwell would be most happy to go out, on an honorary basis, and help in the forwarding of the new project which was to be along lines he had advocated for many years. Such an offer was profoundly moving and almost equally perplexing! There were considerable risks, whether of age, or of military and political uncertainty, or of adaptability to new conditions. Would one be justified in accepting this splendid offer? And when I spoke of the possibility of death out there, Dr. Maxwell said that there was no land he would sooner die in than the country he had served for so long.

The offer was accepted by Council; and in a last note scribbled before he and Mrs. Maxwell joined their ship at Liverpool early in 1949, he wrote to me: " We do hope that we shan't let the Mission down. That and not the Communists is all that worries us." They certainly did not " let the Mission down ". On the contrary, they moved into Hangchow just three weeks before the Communist armies, and went to reside in quarters up at the Leprosy Hospital. " *Please* don't worry about us or let the Council worry. Here we are and here we remain unless we are actually kicked out, which seems unlikely. And if anything should happen to us we are in the Lord's hands and are content." For a short time they were cut off at the Leprosy Hospital during the change-over of government. " We have not been out of this compound for ten days. That really is not any great deprivation as there are lovely walks on the hillside." Dr. Maxwell at once got down to the detailed examination of the sixty patients : " I am at the same time making notes of each patient as regards his fitting into work in the new settlement "; he began to learn the local dialect, and waited for opportunity to help, with Dr. Sturton of the C.M.S. Hospital in the city, in more directly forwarding the Zang-peh project.

Plans went forward rather like a ship in heavy weather which has to change its course and sail, but by doing so makes progress in spite of uncertain winds. Buildings, temporary or more permanent, went up. Mr. Dzen, the Chinese friend who had made his great offer, worked himself till his health broke down under the strain. But other friends arose. And on December 29th, 1949, a cable came : " Twenty lepers installed Zang-peh happily." The nucleus of a new centre of fellowship was established.

And in those first days it was very largely a Christian fellowship of patients transferred from the Hangchow Home. Other patients also came from surrounding villages, and became enquirers and learners about the Faith. Dr. Sturton wrote of a most moving celebration of Holy Communion in which he shared. It was held in the seed and farm tool store. " There was a deep sense of thankfulness and God's presence. I would rather have knelt on the bare floor there than in Westminster Abbey." I am still moved as I think of that development of Christian witness and service in the early days of the People's Government. In circumstances accounted dark and adverse there shone this precious jewel of faith. The authorities were friendly. " The work has certainly won the appreciation of the authorities," wrote Dr. Maxwell, " and they have no desire whatever that we should go." Indeed, they soon began to take an active and, as was to be expected, a controlling share. But as numbers of patients grew into hundreds, the Christian stamp remained upon the work; and it even became possible to build a Christian chapel, which was dedicated by the Bishop early in 1952. Funds for this were largely given by an Ulster friend of The Mission to Lepers who, though we warned him of the uncertain situation, splendidly contributed, confident with the insight of faith that there could be no finer purpose for his gift.

On August 8th, 1951, Dr. Maxwell fell ill with a severe attack of malaria and on the afternoon of the 10th he died in the C.M.S. Hospital at Hangchow to which he had been taken. Mrs. Maxwell, who had so gallantly shared in his work all along, was with him at the end. He had finished his course; he had kept the faith.

In a note that I wrote for *The Times* I said :—

". . . In a letter I had from him, written only a week before his death, he wrote of the good results, and of the teaching he was giving to a Chinese doctor to succeed him. ' We have about done all we can here.' In all his letters he revealed his unwavering love of the Chinese people and his desire to serve them. His life was a demonstration of that Christian initiative which meets suffering and evil with goodness and with service.

" On January 1 of this year he wrote to me : ' We wonder what 1951 holds for us. But we are very content to leave that in the Lord's hands and push on as much as we can. Fifty years today since I first reached China and goodness and mercy have followed us all the days of our lives.' Here was the happy Christian warrior, who goes even beyond the front line, makes all he meets his friends, and in the end lays down his life for them."

Government officials in Hangchow attended his funeral and sent flowers; and the Central People's Government in Peking, in an obituary notice, paid tribute in *The People's China* to his great services and friendship for the people, a most unusual act at that time. The new institution at Zang-peh came more and more to be a demonstra-

tion centre to show that the new government was
determined to deal with the leprosy problem in a way
which previous governments had neglected to do; and
the last news of it, before silence fell beyond the bamboo
curtain, was of plans to develop it for 2,000 patients. The
last letter we received was from Dr. Sturton in the summer
of 1952, by which time all patients had been moved from
Hangchow to the new argricultural settlement, and
government had taken charge.

" The lepers are now all out at Zang-peh and Hsa
Peh (an adjoining additional site). Dr. Yao, the new
superintendent, is providing them with a former temple
hall at Hsa Peh so that they can have a chapel there
also.

" He has decided to put Maxwell's bookcase in the
chapel at Zang-peh, with his urn on it, his portrait
behind it, and to have flowers kept on it perpetually.
I think it is a very nice decision.

" Dr. Yao has a staff of eight doctors now and expects
to expand to 2,000 beds in 1953, as against the present
total of 400. In 1947 we little dreamed that we were
founding such a leper colony."

I have never read a more touching and understanding
letter of fellowship at a time of sorrow than the one which
the patients at Zang-peh sent to Mrs. Maxwell immediately they heard of Dr. Maxwell's death. I think it is
one of quite splendid significance in revealing what the
service of compassion does in building the strong arch of
fellowship between nation and nation, man and man.

" Dear Mistress Maxwell,

" We are extremely sorrowful and mournful to hear
the news, brought by Dr. Kao who came here, Zang-peh,
this morning, that Dr. Maxwell, stricken in age, known
of virtue, zealous and earnest in helping us all his life,
has gone out of this world, being received in Heaven by

God. We are so pained in our hearts because we can no longer see him, who ever loved us with the full love of the Lord Christ.

" We pray that the Lord will kindly receive his spirit to sit in Paradise above. Amen.

" Oh, dear Mistress Maxwell, we say you are so kind and so understanding a lady as just can not work out a wrong way of thinking. That is to say that you are even right to be over mourned at Doctor Maxwell's going; but, we think we are likewise not wrong to ask you not to be so, but carefully preserve your own body. It would be rather an importance and also a difficulty to you. However, we are sure that you are able to overcome it for God strengthens you and comes to your aid always every moment.

" Now all of us, who has been bathing in both you and Dr. Maxwell's grace and love, being not able to do anything as a reward, write this letter to you with immeasurable gratefulness both in memory of Dr. Maxwell and in consolation for you.

" With best wishes and blessings from

Yours lovingly,

All the inmates of Zang-peh Leprosarium."

VIII

What has all this to do with The Isle of Happy Healing? In one way, nothing; but in another way a great deal, as I shall presently show.

When the Mission found its opportunities of service on the mainland of China diminishing, and heard of the problems which beset the Government of Hong Kong by reason of the sharp increase of its own leprosy problem which accompanied the influx of a million and more refugees, among whom were substantial numbers with leprosy, it felt it must act. And in October, 1950, it gave authority and encouragement to Dr. Neil Fraser, its Medical Secretary for China and Hong Kong, to address himself to this problem and to assure the Government of the Mission's readiness to help substantially, provided such help did not weaken a sense of responsibility in government circles and among the public, and that their support also was enlisted. With this lead Dr. Fraser went to work with an energy which matched his enthusiasm, and which created in a remarkably short while the foundations of what today is a notable example of fruitful co-operative action issuing from the warm fellowship of those moved by a common concern for people in need. Dr. Fraser began by giving help where he could. Government had already gathered together some leprosy victims in an annexe of the Tung Wah Hospital, but they were receiving no treatment. Then they were removed to some huts built beside a remote beach, Sandy Bay. It was at this stage that Dr. Fraser began his work, introducing modern treatment, and by a personal concern bringing the beginnings of hope. Although proper accommodation was only built for seventy, there were soon two hundred patients in residence. Out-patient work was engaged in, and on a small scale survey work; and it was very evident that something much more comprehensive and permanent was required. Sites on the island of Hong Kong were looked at; but as soon at it was known that the purpose was a leprosy institution, a resistance movement was set up and purchase became impossible. Finally, government offered an empty island, formerly sparsely populated, but deserted because it was without a water supply, and there appeared to be no resources for securing one in the dry season. It was nine miles from the island of Hong Kong, beautifully situated, but barren and uninhabited, save for a handful of transient fishermen who used its beaches.

It is at this point that the whole enterprise takes on a story-like quality. It was now the summer of 1951. A Hong Kong Auxiliary of the Mission had been formed, and was blessed with leaders who gave the utmost support to Dr. Fraser. Should government's offer of a whole island, one and a half miles long and half a mile broad, for the peppercorn rent of HK$10.00 a year (15s. in British currency) be accepted? Would it only be buying trouble? Nine miles of water to cross, nothing on the island to constitute a base for beginning, no assured supply of water. It seemed that all the weight of common-sense reasoning was against acceptance of the offer. However, two small springs were found, one high up in the hills, the other nearer to one of the beaches. That brought the beginnings of hope, and it was decided to accept Government's offer.

The island was called Nun Island; but now in faith it was renamed *Hay Ling Chau,* the Isle of Happy Healing. It is quite impossible here to tell the story of how the change of name came to be justified in fact as the enterprise went forward. It is certainly a story which should be told some day, for it is full of romance, a story of courage and wonderful co-operation. From among his 200 patients at Sandy Bay, Dr. Fraser called for pioneers. It must always be remembered that leprosy sufferers are made up of all sorts of people, good and bad, co-operative and complaining. Dr. Fraser had a fair share of all. But twenty-two of the most willing patients who themselves were not advanced cases volunteered. And then there came the day, at the very end of July, 1951, when, with Dr. Fraser, they crossed in a launch to the empty island, with their bundles of belongings, boxes of food supplies, and tools to work with. Temporary shelters were quickly put up, and the work was begun. Ten days before Dr. Maxwell fell ill in Hangchow and died, these other pioneers began their labour of building a new enterprise of healing and fellowship.

An early need was to build up a water-supply. The first patients used water from the small spring near the beach, but it was seen that the main supply for the future must come from the hills. A catchment area below the upper spring was a first need, into which the water from the spring would be channelled, and into which other water during the rainy periods would flow. It was here that British soldiers in the Engineers and other regiments played their part. They offered spare-time help, especially in laying pipes to bring down the water to the building area below. Chinese merchants and others helped with supplies. The soldiers would come in batches for weekends, camping out and fraternising with the first patients down below, and doing their bit to help the project go forward.

Now, only two years and six months after the first patients had landed, my wife and I, on a sunny, placid sea, were going to the island on the launch *Ling Hong*—the Spirit of Healing on the Waters. We were to be there for a nine-day stay, during which the main formal occasion would be the opening of the Maxwell Memorial Medical Centre.

As we approached the island all looked deserted until we came round a headland. There was only rough brown scrub, sharply-rising low hills, narrow fringes of sand between rocky coves and the languid sea. But when we had rounded the headland we saw a company of men and women and children waiting for us on a jetty; and behind them a long one-storeyed building, delightfully proportioned, and with a gaily-painted moon doorway as its central feature. This was the first building to be erected, serving as living quarters, workshop, stores, office, everything. When we landed we were received with grave and courteous and bowing welcomes by the 320 patients, and with more informality by a small and diverse staff. Part of the one-hundredth Psalm was sung for us by the children, and soon we were climbing a hill, past beauti-fully-tended vegetable gardens, and then past a lacquer-red and green open summer-house used for small meetings and choir practices. This was a personal memorial build-ing given by members of Dr. Fraser's family in honour of their parents. The view widened and we looked across blue waters to other islands, and to the mainland, with the mountain of Lantau, a deep grape-purple, wearing a pale scarf of grey clouds around its shoulders. And then, entering the staff bungalow, China tea refreshed us as we talked and admired the skill and beauty and simplicity of this building, with its friendly common room, and its dining-room with a kitchen on one side and a staff chapel on the other. I liked that arrangement, of such happy significance. And beyond, like arms extended on either side, ran rows of small bedrooms, where the whole team of workers—Chinese, Scottish, English, Canadian—lived. The guest rooms had a constant procession of visitors, three or four National Service soldiers coming regularly in turn every weekend, glad to get away from barracks for this home life, and given by Dr. Fraser some little job to do, so that they also became temporary members of the team. Later we were to see all the various buildings which have gone up, some by the patients' labour, and others by contract. Pleasant cottages had been built, placed at various strategic points, so that the patients could develop different parts of the island. And what has been achieved by them is quite amazing, in field cultivation, gardening, road-making, a thriving fishing industry, and handicrafts. And, still empty and closed, with feverish finishing touches being done to doors and cupboards, was the splendid new Maxwell Memorial Medical Centre.

It is typical of the spirit of co-operation shown by friends in Hong Kong that this and the other buildings were designed without fee by a Hong Kong architect, Mr. G. A. Hall. Here, in this island enterprise, one saw that broadening of the normal missionary society enterprise into a Christian community one. For the extensive building programme government gave substantial help; and so did the people of Hong Kong. And for the maintenance of the work, public and private sources have combined together in effective co-operation. At a reception which was held for us at Hong Kong I was able to say " Thank you " to at least some of the many friends, too numerous to mention by name. From the Bishop and the Dean, with a varied array of denominational leaders and representatives of the Salvation Army, the company extended to government officials, social workers, business and professional men, ladies' groups of helpers, both Chinese and European. These ladies' groups have done remarkable work, as illustrated by their colouring by hand of 10,000 Christmas cards for sale, their hard work for a Christmas Fair, their help on a most productive Flag Day. There were " exiled " missionaries present also who at various times and in various ways have helped in service on the island. The arch of fellowship was indeed very manifest at that happy gathering.

And it was even more manifest on the day when the

A Bridge of Compassion

Maxwell Memorial Medical Centre was opened by the Governor, Sir Alexander Grantham, accompanied by Lady Grantham. For in this the patients also shared; as did friends in many parts of the British Commonwealth who had given liberally to supply funds for the building. They shared very directly, even though they could not be present. A special steamer was chartered, and over 200 friends of many nationalities came over from Hong Kong and Kowloon to take part in the great occasion. Mr. O. Skinner, the chairman of the Hong Kong Auxiliary, and Mrs. Skinner, received the guests. One cannot estimate the value to the work of the devotion and experience of this warm-hearted and wise gentleman.

The building has a beauty, a spaciousness, and a comprehensive character, which made their immediate appeal to the visitors. There are hospital wards, treatment rooms, laboratories, facilities for autopsies, X-ray rooms, dispensary, stores, offices. Dr. Olaf Skinsnes, a would-be China missionary diverted to Hong Kong and now a pathologist at the Hong Kong University, gave much time to co-operating with Dr. Fraser and Mr. Hall the architect in planning the requirements of this Centre. Now that it is in use, medical students from Hong Kong come over in turn to gain practical experience in leprosy and its treatment. And in the wards men and women receive all the skilled care and friendship they need. There is a team of Chinese nurses, with Miss Irene Moore, a Canadian missionary, leading them : some are fully qualified; others are patients learning as they work. There is a Chinese lady doctor. And now there is Dr. H. Jocelyn Smyly, a veteran English missionary doctor who volunteered to go out and help. How great is the advance from the imaginative improvisations with which Dr. Fraser courageously began to work in Hong Kong only three years before the day of the opening of this Memorial building!

While we were at the Isle of Happy Healing, my wife, amid all the many engagements which enriched our brief stay, whether in Hong Kong churches, or at social gatherings, or with the patients at worship, somehow managed to " shoot " a ciné film, which has since been produced in sound and colour with great success. It is a documentary film, based directly on the autobiographical account of his life by one of the patients.* Helped by Miss Rachael Bennett, the missionary social worker on the island who stood at her side to translate and give directions, and with the ready co-operation of patients who had arranged some of the scenes, this authentic story of a single patient graphically depicts the transformation from despair to hope, and loneliness to fellowship which the Isle of Happy Healing has made possible. How my wife, without even the aid of a tripod for her camera, and moving under the hot sun for hours at a stretch, managed to secure this film I do not know; for without studio facilities, or the opportunity to see how the shots had turned out until months later, it was a case of now or never every time she released the trigger of her Kodak.

I will not in this chapter write of the central religious faith and fervour which has been at the heart of this island enterprise because I want to touch upon this when we come to the next chapter. Here at present we must leave the island, rejoicing at the part it is taking today in witnessing to the character and depth of Christian concern for the individual. Without arms of war it is registering

* *The Story of Cheng-Su*—Sound/Colour : 32 minutes : 16mm.; 16 frames a second.

107

its victories; and with extended arms of service it is bringing the lonely into community. If there are in the Far East other frontiers which bring contention and strife, one may see at the Isle of Happy Healing something of the Kingdom without frontiers, offering its welcome, and bringing its emancipation.

IX

The illustrations I have used in this chapter have been taken entirely from work in the East with which it has been my privilege to have had personal touch. But the reader must remember that equally significant ones can be taken from a much broader range of stations, and from many other lands. Especially perhaps in various countries in the great continent of Africa there have been notable examples of men and women who have made the response of compassion to the needs of leprosy victims, and have with hands outstretched welcomed them and served them. In some parts of the continent government acted ahead of the missionary, but that action ordinarily issued from fear rather than love and had for its primary purpose the protection of the public. Compulsion rather than compassion was its hallmark. It did not help in the building of the arch of fellowship. The warm uniting touch of friendship does not stem from legislative acts of compulsory segregation.

It is when " love casteth out fear " that the great creative deeds of compassion are enacted. When Edith Patton (later Mrs. Moules) went out to the Belgian Congo as a missionary nurse with the Worldwide Evangelization Crusade there was one particular person she prayed she

The new Memorial Church at the Poladpur Home, Bombay.   See pages 120–122

WORSHIP AND THE WORD

Fingerless hands rest upon the pages of St. John's Gospel in Bengali at the Purulia Home.   See pages 122–125

Christian Patients leaving the Church of the Dawn, Nagashima, Japan, February, 1955. See pages 202–204

THE ETERNAL HOPE

Part of the overflow congregation at Pusan, Korea, January, 1955. See pages 144–146

might never have to minister to. Exaggerated or wrong conceptions of leprosy had created in her mind a secret paralyzing fear. And then—how could it be otherwise in the heart of Africa?—there came the occasion when she was confronted with the very person she had prayed she might never meet. At her general dispensary there were some 300 patients that day.

" Suddenly at the back of them all I saw a leper. . . . He was led by a small boy, and was almost naked. His toes and fingers were gone, his feet swollen, no nose and he was dribbling from his lipless mouth down over his bare body. Both he and the child looked travel-stained and hungry. I did not want to touch that man and I said to myself, ' Oh, we cannot have a leper here; but whatever shall I do?' "

Mrs. Moules, in spite of her fears, made temporary provision for the night in an old shack up the hill. She hoped he would go away after a day or two, but he didn't.

" Well, so we went on day after day, that man standing there until everybody else had gone and then saying, ' Haven't you anything for me?' and still that awful shrinking in my heart and the feeling that I did not want to touch him and wishing he would not come. I went to God again and again—and again and again. I could not tell you the hours spent before God those four days, telling Him all about that man, telling Him I was really sorry for the poor leper—but it was not my job. It took me four days to find out that it *was* my job."

Decision came on the fourth night.

" I do not want to be a hypocrite and say that that night I learned that every man is my neighbour and that l now love every man, my neighbour, as myself. I dare not say such a thing; but I did learn that it is the highest at which we have to aim—every day and all day, whether that neighbour is likeable or unlikeable, whether that neighbour praises me or does not praise me. It is

H

because we fail in this that there is trouble and dryness and lack of power in our lives. Over and over again came the command, 'And thy neighbour as thyself'; and it was not until I realized that the leper was *my* neighbour that I could get peace."

From that victory of the spirit sprang deeds of compassion which set in motion not only a leprosy camp at Nebobongo, later to be replaced by work at Malingwia, and a large children's hostel, but also a growing network of new enterprises which owe their direct origin to the burning and yearning enthusiasm of Mrs. Moules to broaden out this service into other areas of unmet need. After her husband's early death, and a doctor's warning that her own time on earth was very limited, she spent herself in a " leprosy crusade ", as she called it, under the auspices of the W.E.C., recruiting, raising funds, negotiating with government authorities in the Gold Coast, Liberia, Senegal, Portuguese Guinea and the Ivory Coast, building the foundations of new work in the short time left to her before her gallant spirit was released from her body's suffering. I recall Mrs. Moules now, with sheaves of papers in her hands, talking eagerly to me of her plans *after* the doctor's verdict had been given, determined to work till all strength was gone in facing the challenge she had at first sought to evade—" Who is my neighbour?"*

And then what a mighty work has arisen within the mission field of the Church of Scotland at Itu in Calabar, near to where Mary Slessor established a hospital fifty years ago. There Dr. A. B. Macdonald laboured, and he has told† of the challenge which came to him when one

* *Mighty Through God.* Published by the Lutterworth Press. Price 5s. 6d.

† *Can Ghosts Arise?* Published by the Church of Scotland, Edinburgh. Price 5s.

man with leprosy came to his general dispensary in 1926. He had no chaulmoogra oil, but secured some from London, and soon instead of one man 400 were being treated. They came from long distances and built for themselves shelters on a sandbank until Dr. Macdonald secured a proper site and began the organization of today's widely-famed institution. Costs were kept to a minimum by developing a palm-oil industry, derelict machinery and a steam-engine from an abandoned steamer being brought in to make an oil-press. Numbers increased into thousands, and a vigorous community life was developed; there were schools, markets, a town band, a library, scouts and guides, crafts, and at the heart of it all the Church life, with a place for worship which regularly had a congregation of 2,000 people. The transformation at Itu of a waste site into a township of happy citizens, made up of men and women who come lonely and fearful, and in time go away renewed and full of joy, is a signal evidence of the emancipating power of Christian fellowship.

A more recent example, and one with which this chapter may fitly close, is the present rapid development of leprosy work at Lambarene in the French Gabon. Lambarene will ever be associated with the name of Dr. Albert Schweitzer, and the general hospital he established there was deliberately an act of outgoing friendship, an effort to heal not only broken bodies but help atone for the wrongs which the exploitation of trading and political power had inflicted on defenceless and backward people. To that hospital, which represented such a strange conjunction of the primitive and the advanced, there came the typical wrecks of humanity who were the worst victims of leprosy, hoping that " le grand docteur " would do something for them. In his reverence for life, he had reverence for these men also. Always ready to improvise and not allow the absence of desirable equipment to hinder the operation of human kindness, he made rough provision for cases in greatest need within the general compound. And then, when the sulphone drugs began to give encouraging results, larger numbers, including less advanced cases, began to appear. In 1950 there were between fifty and sixty leprosy patients only, housed in temporary bamboo huts. The numbers increased to 100 in 1951, 200 in 1952, and 300 in 1953. Dr. Schweitzer was now seventy-eight, but without hesitation he faced the task of building a separate and more permanent village, with the labour of the patients as far as possible, but with his own as well. The musician, the theologian, the doctor, the missionary, was also carpenter, mason, and foreman.

" The village has had to be built with the labour of the inmates who are able to work, and those lepers whose general state of health is more or less satisfactory. And since I am the only one with the authority to keep them at the job I have to be my own contractor again.

" Moreover, I regard it as a matter of principle that those who find shelter and care in this Hospital maintained by gifts should serve it with the labour of which they are capable, and so acknowledge what they are receiving.

" So now again, in my old age, as once before in 1925 to 1927 when the new Hospital was being built, I have the satisfaction of being able to offer the sick incomparably better shelter than before as a result of building operations which I have undertaken. But this satisfaction cannot entirely make up for the fact that while the building is going on I have to lead an entirely different life from what I intended."

In a letter I had from him written in March, 1954,

he wrote, in his even handwriting which looks so un-hurried, so calm (the original is in French) :—

"I am anxious to thank you for the precious gift that The Mission to Lepers has sent to me again this year. I am touched by your sympathy with my work. You tell of your interest in the building of the village for the lepers. I send you herewith a small photograph which shows the debris of one of the old bamboo huts and in the background the new huts. It has been a very difficult job because it was necessary first of all to prepare the site for the hospital on the summit of a small hill. The new buildings are on the side of a road which runs the length of the site. The huts stand on a little cement wall and have a framework of hardwood and corrugated iron roofs. The walls of the huts are just bark. Two patients share a room. I have built to be able to house 200 patients. The village is surrounded by tall trees and oil palms. Fortunately, the Nobel Peace Prize has enabled me to make purchases of cement and hard timber to complete the village."

How appropriate that this man of peace should use part of the Nobel Peace Prize to provide further wood and cement to bring peace to African tribesmen who before had known the enmity of kinsmen because of their afflic-tion! Dr. Schweitzer has set an example of obedience to the demand which compassion makes, that it should always issue in practical action. In his Nobel Peace Prize address at Stockholm, he spoke of " compassion, in which all ethics must take root ". Therein is the dynamic power of what is being done at Lambarene. The convictions of a profound mind have become incarnate at a wayside river halt on the edge of the primeval forest. There the building of the bridge of compassion is going on, and its reach is world-wide. Friendship and peace between all men is promoted by the simple arch of fellowship built for a few hundred African victims of leprosy by an Alsace doctor and his colleagues who follow the way of Christ's compassion, and by the aid which goes to them from men of goodwill and Christian faith in many lands.

And what is happening at Lambarene is repeated at many another remote centre of friendly welcome and service. The unresisted co-existence of health and sickness, community life for some and isolation for others, knowledge and ignorance, freedom and servitude, this is intolerable in the Christian society. Co-existence must be overcome by co-operation and by the transformation of human relationships on to a new plane of mutual respect and service. One can but thank God that in this transformation the service of sufferers from leprosy, issuing from the Christian's faith in the worth of every man, is in our time and generation playing so striking a part.

THE ARCH OF ETERNAL HOPE

I

It is a very incomplete service of the man in need which does not include the dimension of eternity. In the depths of his heart every man knows that physical and social good alone cannot give him fulness of life. And if this is so for those who are healthy and have plenty of friends, how much more is it true for those suffering from leprosy! For them a service which brings no spiritual comfort or insight is a sadly deficient one. This is self-evident in the case of the victim hopelessly maimed by the disease; but it is not perhaps so immediately clear in the case of the man who comes for help while he has only early symptoms, with every prospect of recovering with the aid of modern treatment. Yet he runs the greater peril of looking for his total good in physical health and social security. It is one of the paramount dangers of our age of technological mastery and the application of scientific findings to the enrichment of the temporal life of man that he may come to look for his whole fulfilment in possessions from which at the last his grip must loosen. It would indeed be a tragedy if the Christian service of sufferers from leprosy lost the clear call to fellowship with God and healing from the diseases of the soul just because the opportunities of bringing physical healing and social rehabilitation have increased. Then it would itself succumb to the modern malady of counting temporal gains greater than eternal ones.

A Bridge of Compassion

It has been a high privilege of The Mission to Lepers that from its earliest days it has been able to strengthen the hands of those who have sought to bring the challenge and comfort of the Gospel to their patients. In the Bible which Mr. Wellesley Bailey used in the early days of the Mission he inserted a number of pages for reference which revealed how deeply he was concerned for the spiritual peace and victory of the men and women he visited at the first Homes to be helped by the Mission. One entry tells of Musuwa, a patient at Almora whom he believed to be the first convert to Christianity in any of the Homes in India established as a consequence of Christian compassion.

" Dear old Musuwa was one of the lepers which were befriended nearly fifty years ago by the present Hon. Sir H. Ramsay. At the time of the establishment of the present Institution in 1850 (on admission roll of which Musuwa's name stands second) he was about twenty-five years of age, having been a leper for at least five years. During these forty-six years he suffered less or more from the ravages of the disease. He was one of the cases on which the gurjun oil treatment was tried, and at times, and for a long time together it seemed as if the disease had been arrested, but alas! again and again, it showed by virulent outburst that it had only been lying latent in the system.

" Mr. Hewlett wrote to me on hearing of the old man's death, ' The news takes me back to that January afternoon in 1864, the day which in many respects is the most affecting in my memory, when on the spot where the Leper Chapel now stands I gathered the inmates of the Asylum and spoke to them lovingly of the Great Physician who could heal all their woes, and on appealing to them to entrust themselves to His mercy, was delighted beyond measure to see Musuwa, who did not then appear to be a young man, stand up and say, with face and hands upturned to heaven, " Since Jesus has done so much for me, how can I help doing whatever He requires of me?" His declaring himself on this occasion on the Saviour's side led to his baptism together with that of two others whom he had persuaded to join him in following Christ, on Sunday morning, Almora, Feb. 14th, 1864, in the Mission Church.'

" He was blind for the last twenty-four years, as the result of the terrible ravages of the disease with which he was so sadly afflicted. Yet this defect did not seem in any way to detract from his power to influence others, or lessen the zeal he manifested in doing good. He might well be called the leper missionary to lepers. . . . He was always full of gladness, spiritual joy beamed out of his ' beloved leprous face ' and never once did I hear him complain. On the contrary, he seemed to be continually praising God for His goodness and love, and thanking and praying for the friends of lepers who had done so much to alleviate the miseries of those afflicted like himself.

" He died on Sept. 4th, 1891, surrounded by a number of his more particular friends amongst the lepers, and his last words to them were : ' I am going to Jesus, do you continue to walk in His ways '."

II

Since that first known convert a great company of fellow-believers has arisen in Leprosy Homes associated with the Mission. And again and again it has been the story of Jesus Christ, in all its simplicity and sublimity, which has brought light and penitence and trust and devotion. The sufferer from leprosy is not perplexed with questions of Biblical authorship or of church order, but he is by his own misfortunes; and he, in common with all men, is also faced with the fact of his own sinfulness, and his personal need. " Who shall deliver me from the body

117

of this death?" is a cry which carries a double significance for the man smitten with leprosy. And when he finds in experience that Jesus Christ is his Deliverer he becomes a new man.

Those of us who have been privileged to see the imparted life of Christ at work in patients know how the Church in a Leprosy Home (not the building but the fellowship of believers) is its salt and its light. The evangelical fervour of the pioneer founders of Homes enabled them to offer a more lasting medicine than any which could be issued from the dispensary counter. My mind ranges back to some of the congregations with whom it has been my joy to share in the praise of God. I think of an Easter Day in the little hilltop church at Chandag Heights, the snow mountains of Nepal so clear on the horizon, with Mary Reed present, herself both superintendent and patient, and the crippled but devoted women singing together, " Jesus Christ is risen today, *Alleluia* !". I think of a forest leprosy colony at Saldoha in the Santal Parganas, with a long line of peasant patients moving up the centre aisle of the large sunlit church to lay their simple offerings of eggs and vegetables upon the holy table. They were to help support the evangelistic work of the Church. When I had visited the colony while it was being built in 1923, the area was entirely unevangelized. It was healed patients going back to their villages who were the messengers of good tidings, and the means of establishing village Churches. I think of a heap of thrown-out bricks and rubble, and a slim Indian doctor sitting on it at the end of the day of the opening of a new Home at Vadathorasalur in South India. Seated there he told the first half-dozen patients a simple story about a Good Physician called Jesus, Whose very name they had to learn. A little later in this chapter we shall return to that Home and meet this doctor again thirty years later. And then I think of a group of Chinese patients, gathered as close as possible to a central stove which was repeatedly fed with fresh fuel, at the Home in Langchow above the half-frozen Yellow River. Their knowledge of Scripture was astonishing; their bulky Bibles were soiled and worn with use; one of the patients prayed in a language of which I knew no word, and yet the simplicity and earnestness of his speech caught me up into a sharing of his act of adoration. Or I think of a church building at Moulmein in a Home away in Burma, with half the roof blown off by bombs, where I sat listening to the patients singing anthems of praise to their Redeemer. I think of services in many parts of India, where patients, whether in stream or baptistry, have declared their faith in Jesus Christ as Saviour and Lord. And I think of those many hundreds and thousands of patients with whom I have knelt and stood during the years, whether in Anglican or Presbyterian or Baptist or Methodist or Lutheran churches which the Mission has provided in Leprosy Homes, or at the assembly of Brethren, and shared with them the emblems of remembrance of " the Lord's death, till He come ". These are great experiences, indelibly impressed on the heart. They tell of the arch of eternal hope, well built, and men moving joyously across it, pilgrims to a better land. Truly Christ's Church among these folk is the " Fellowship of the Tenth Leper ", made up of those who have returned to glorify God at the feet of the Master, even though physical healing may not be vouchsafed to them.

And beyond those who of their own conviction and free-will join the visible company of declared disciples there is a still greater number of patients who recognize their debt to Christ while not joining the Christian Church. The Mission to Lepers has a zealous concern that there should be no sort of favouritism for the Christian, and no inducements to make a change of profession of faith. We may desire or pray for this; but we must gratefully recognize the operation of God's redeeming love in the changed lives of many who do not enter into the full obligations of church membership. I have seen Christ's spirit manifestly at work in the life of many a patient who knows Him, sings His praises, finds in His Cross the answer to his need, tries to follow Him in unselfish living, and yet does not join His Church. This may be disappointing for those who long for all men to enter into the full commitments of Christian discipleship; but we must be ready to thank God that in these days when so many more patients are discharged and able to resume life in the general community they go back friends of the Gospel, able to tell their neighbours something of the transforming friendship of Christ.

III

During the tour I have recently made I was again able to share in many acts of worship in the Homes visited. I must mention but a few, so various in setting and form, but so identical at heart. Only a day after we arrived at Bombay we bounced our way over execrable roads to Poladpur, to share in the fiftieth anniversary rejoicings of the founding of this now stalwart community of patients, and centre of healing. Part of the celebrations was a well-acted record by the patients of the coming of Christian messengers to Poladpur and of the way in which this work began. First they showed Donald Mitchell, Scotland's first missionary to India, dying by the wayside outside the village, away back in 1823, and offering his dying prayer that though he fell the message he brought might reach the hearts of the people and live in them. Then there followed the years of inactivity and seeming failure until Haripant Kelkar, Brahmin convert and schoolmaster, came to Poladpur, saw the condition of leprosy victims, and in great humanity began to build for them a bridge of compassion. The story has been told of how he begged and built, till there was a tiny colony of rough huts for those homeless folk, with one for himself just across the road. How well the patients portrayed the change which came as the message of eternal hope was told them, and chiefly, perhaps, sung to them in lovely Marathi religious lyrics by this great man of God! Such was the beginning in 1893 of the present Poladpur Home. Soon after The Mission to Lepers had taken over Haripant Kelkar's financial cares and provided a proper site and buildings, the patients built their own first simple chapel of wood and thatch; then there followed an open-sided structure with iron roof which has served for many years. And now, during these fiftieth anniversary celebrations, came the afternoon when the tower of the new memorial church was dedicated to God. A photograph of this new church appears facing page 108, and the tower which it was my privilege to declare as built and offered for the glory of God stands out above the Home and is a land-mark for many miles around. Poladpur is in a well-wooded valley set among surrounding hills; and whether one travels up to Mahableshwar, or along the southern road towards Goa, this white finger points upward above the green trees. The tower is so designed that it serves

many purposes. Unseen from outside there is, to begin
with, a vestry and study for the leader of the worship, a
place for quiet and spiritual refreshment; and then above
that a storage tank for the circulation of water throughout
the Home. The tower therefore represents the supply by
God of both our physical and spiritual needs. And then,
higher up, and visible to all, is the great clock, and above
that the belfry; again a happy combination—the call of
the clock to heed and make good the fleeting hours of
Time, and the call of the bells to heed and serve the
Eternal God. Finally, crowning all, is the bare and empty
Cross, supreme sign both of God's sacrifice and of His
victory.

As I talked with Professor Fraser and Dr. Das (and
was there ever a happier partnership in service by men
of different race?), I asked if they had put in a lightning
conductor.

" Oh, yes," they said.

" Where is it? I can't see any signs of it," I replied.

" No, you can't because it is concealed in the Cross,
and runs down from inside it deep into the ground below."

I was delighted that there was this further symbolism;
Christ's vicarious bearing away in Himself of man's peril
and doom. It proclaimed the *inwardness* of the Cross.
I thought of all the attacks of Satan's lightnings without,
and the worshipping company within of those whose trust
is in God's redeeming love incarnate in Christ; and over
them the Cross, and Christ bearing away in His offered
Body the enmity and destruction of the Evil One. Here
was the substance of their eternal hope.

A few weeks later I was at the Church of the Good
Samaritan, set in the centre of the Mission's great Home
and Hospital at Purulia in Bihar. It was the Sunday of

Harvest Festival, a great event at this Home which is surrounded by rice fields cultivated by the patients. Every stage of cultivation is made an occasion for praise and prayer—the plantings of the first seeds in the heat of summer; the transplantation of the first seedlings in the monsoon rains; the cutting of the first ripe grain under the winter sunshine; and now the offering of thanks for the ingathered harvest. There is a happy vying of house with house in the making of generous offerings at the festival service. For months patients have put aside a little of their week's allowance of uncooked rice; they have made paper-enclosed rolls of slowly-saved *pice*, or farthings, which, like Joseph hiding treasure in the sacks, they have put in their wide wicker baskets of grain. They come to the church—which is gaily decorated with marigold festoons, and plaited ears of corn, and vegetables from their gardens—bearing these baskets on their heads and singing to the beat of drums and clash of cymbals. They are men and women who have lost all introspection, all loneliness, as they share in the chief aim of man, " to glorify God and to enjoy Him for ever ". In the celebration of thanksgiving for temporal mercies they find eternal treasure. Their joy is in the Lord.

Here at Purulia I need no interpreter, for Bengali is the Indian language I learned; and though my remembrance of it is rusty I am able to speak to the happy congregation in their own tongue. As I look around I think of other harvests at the Home during the years that are gone, not only of rice but of men and women. There was a time when there were some 400 communicant members of the church, and when we had to add transepts to the building, for Sunday after Sunday there were congregations of over 700 people. Today there is a greater hesitance to cut formally adrift from the Hindu fold; the prospect of return to the general community, set within the framework of caste distinction and having no welcome for the man who has cut himself off from his past traditions, is a dismaying one, even with physical health regained. But even now there are those who have the courage to make the clear step, for all to see.

Among the congregation was a man wearing the saffron-coloured garment which denotes, to the Indian, dedication to the religious life. He was a highly-educated patient called Shashibhusan Patnaik. Of good family, he had, after leaving college, followed the life of a Hindu *sanyasi,* or holy man, travelling to many pilgrim centres and seeking spiritual emancipation. He found leprosy developing in his body and after trying many " quack " medicines got in touch with Dr. Muir at the time he was back at Purulia, helping the Mission tide over a period of shortage in medical leadership. Mr. Patnaik was admitted to the Home, where he continued his religious exercises and studies while he received treatment. He found a friendship and good cheer among the staff and patients which made him interested in the Christian faith. Had it the answer to his quest? He asked for a Bible and studied it. Mr. William Bailey was superintendent of the Home at the time, and with his encouragement he explored further, attending a Bible class for English-speaking patients and reading commentaries. He began to co-operate in various activities of the Home, helping organize a glazed pottery industry, and supervising the communal kitchen. He was still a Hindu at the time of my visit, but a very eager member of the congregation which met for Christian worship. And then, a few months later, he made declaration of his faith in Christ to a group of non-

Christian patients, and took the courageous step of asking for baptism. Mr. Bailey was now on furlough, and wrote to Mr. Patnaik to express his happiness. This is the letter Mr. Bailey received in reply : —

" There is nothing to be astonished at in my sudden change, as nothing is impossible for Him. At an instant He turned water into wine; at an instant He drove out the evil spirit; at an instant He healed the sick. His very grace makes the impossible possible; the inaccessible accessible. His mercy and mercy alone made me to believe beyond doubt that the Lord Jesus is the one and only Redeemer and Saviour of the world. And no man can reach the Kingdom of God but through Him. There is one God and one mediator between God and man, the Man Christ Jesus."

Since then this new disciple has become a great strength to the Christian work and worship at the Church of the Good Samaritan where, on that December morning, I had seen him as a Hindu enquirer sharing in the harvest festival.

IV

And after Harvest Festival, Christmas. By now my wife and I were down in the south of India at the Vadathorasalur Home and Hospital. We had looked forward to sharing with staff and patients the joys of this lovely time. No longer was a heap of broken bricks required to supply the doctor with a pulpit ! Now, thirty years after that evening which I have a little earlier referred to, we met, not with half a dozen untreated and hungry victims of leprosy who heard a young physician telling them a Gospel story for the first time in their lives, but with a company of over 200 patients who, in their

125

exquisitely-kept church, joined understandingly and with humble devotion in the carols and prayers and praise. The young doctor—Dr. Annaswamy Rao—was now no longer young; from that first day till this he has continued in his Christian service and witness. A few years after the opening of the Home he was joined by Miss E. Lillelund, a missionary nursing sister of the Danish Missionary Society, and since then they have together laboured with unfailing devotion, complementing one another's gifts. Here, during the years, a vigorous Christian Church has been built up, of real influence in the district round about. Indeed, on one of the five days while we were there, there was a baptismal service led by the Indian Lutheran pastor at which not only a few patients made profession of their faith, but also a man from a neighbouring village, his relatives attending in full force.

How delightful it was to see the children with leprosy just bubbling with good spirits as they entered the church for the Christmas celebration! Boys in mustard-yellow shirts, with new maroon scarves over their shoulders. Girls in long voluminous royal blue skirts, and embroidered white blouses. Tiny children in cotton check frocks. The women wearing dark plum-coloured saris. The men in white. From the ceiling hung a criss-cross pattern of paper festoons, rustling in the breeze. The brass on the holy table shone with prolonged polishing. The staff and their families sat in the transepts, the ladies gay in their very best saris. All of us, seated cross-legged on the ground, were one family, praising God for His most precious Gift. At the end came the patients' offerings, so gladly given, coins and live chickens and eggs and vegetables and articles made by the patients. And after that there came, out in the sunshine, the bestowal of gifts from far-away lands. Friends in Denmark and England and Australia and Canada had sent their tokens of love, reminders that the family to which we now belonged was world-wide in its range. My wife busily took ciné shots for a children's film, *The Offering.** Later, we moved to another part of the Home, where the Christmas feast was prepared, and where with " all seated on the ground " curry and rice took the place of turkey and plum pudding. It was significant that poor villagers from round about looked on (having taken care not to forget to bring their bowls with them) and so a part of the heaped food was set aside for them.

On one evening the smaller children rendered for us in the new hospital courtyard a charming narrative of the Nativity in word and song. There were improvised costumes; the recitation of appropriate verses; and significant original touches. It was certainly a truly Eastern touch that when the Wise Men tried to see Herod, the guards took good care to exact their *bakhsheesh,* or tip, before admission to the royal presence was granted ! And then it was the daughter of the innkeeper who had the inspiration to suggest the stable when her father refused admission to the inn; wouldn't a manger make just a perfect cradle ? I remember two other touches, most true to life. After the shepherds had come and gone, women came crowding in to have a look, and surely they must have done that ! And after the solemn procession of the Wise Men came lots of peeping children; and what procession of strange and brightly-clothed people did not have children running after ?

There at Vadathorasalur, in that remote corner of the Madras State, at a spot where a waste site studded with

* *The Offering*—Silent/Colour : 18 minutes : 16 mm.

grey rocks and prickly thorns had been turned into a garden village of hope, Christ, the Hope of the World, was welcomed again by simple peasant folk. Leprosy had first brought them to that place, in need and want; but now they had come together, not as men and women and children sharing a common plight, but as children of God sharing in joy at the great birthday party of the Son, " the firstborn among many brethren ".

There need be no apology for bringing to sufferers from leprosy, in whatever land they live, word of the Christian faith. It steals nothing which has worth. Christ takes nought from a man save the burden of his sin and the chains of his self-centredness. All else He gives; a clear vision of the character of God; an ethical code rooted in the fundamentals of eternal truth; the grace of His own companionship and guidance; the strength of His own freely-given life. Should such a faith offend? And would any withhold from the lonely and dispirited and perplexed this medicine and elixir of the soul?

V

The church buildings at those Homes to which I have just made reference are only three of the scores which have been provided by friends of The Mission to Lepers in many parts of the world, and which proclaim its ecumenical character. To give one instance only, it was at a united meeting held at a Baptist Church in Hamilton, Ontario, that the first nucleus of funds was given for the new Poladpur Leprosy Home Church, which is superintended by a missionary of the Church of Scotland. I had spoken there and told the story of Donald Mitchell and Haripant Kelkar and the growth of the Home, and referred to a cherished hope (it was no more at the time) that a worthy memorial church building might one day go up. There was a liberal collection which came so near to a thousand dollars that the stewards made up the amount on the spot, and I was told that it might be used to begin a fund for the church. Thus encouraged, the project slowly went forward. And at other stations again and again the buildings which have gone up have represented the gifts of those who have not allowed either national or denominational loyalties to narrow the range of their liberality. It is both encouraging and significant that in the immediate twelve months before I write these lines the Mission has been approached to help make it possible for no less than six churches to be built in different leprosy colonies in Africa, to all of which appeals it has been able to make substantial response. And in two other recent cases in India grants for extensions to existing churches have been made. In these various projects the patients themselves have taken their willing share, sacrificing part of their rations month after month, or engaging in the labour of making bricks and helping the masons.

Indeed, there are cases where the whole of the building work has been carried through by patients, and at no place more notably than at the Isle of Happy Healing, about the establishment of which the last chapter told. From the first there were a few Christian patients, with some keen ones among them, and there was also a little later a Chinese Lutheran pastor who was a refugee from the mainland, and who visited them for Bible classes and services of worship. They were held on the hillside, looking down on the pale blue sea. It was not long before a patient went to Dr. Fraser and said, " Doctor, you have a house, and we have houses, but there is no House of God here."

The doctor agreed, but spoke of the many other buildings which must go up before a church building could be contemplated. " But if you patients are ready to build your own church we will do what we can to help you with simple materials." Gladly and eagerly the patients planned their church—stone pillars supporting a simple roof, a wall at one end painted white, with the holy table in front of it, rows of raised planks for the provision of seats; and one or two benches of the conventional kind for staff and visitors. Soon the building was erected. " What shall we call it?" the patients debated. They chose their own lovely and original name in Chinese which, literally translated, means " The Lord Wills Church ". They knew what was the consequence of the Lord Jesus saying, " I will; be thou clean." So they inscribed the name on a white board at the open end of the building, with the cross painted over it in red. And over the communion table they inscribed the Chinese characters for " Glory to God ".

When I joined in the worship at this church I was greatly impressed with the seriousness and enthusiasm of the congregation. The children with leprosy were seated in front, each had an enormous Bible, and unhurried time was given for them to find the passages of reading and text. There was a liturgical framework to the service, with responses in which the congregation joined heartily. The pastor had two interpreters because of the numerous tongues spoken. The offering was received in bags on poles, an old lady and a boy acting as sidesmen. Shortly before our visit there had been a serious fire of refugee huts at Kowloon, and this congregation sacrificially had given out of their bare living allowances HK$300, or about £18 15s., for relief of those rendered homeless once more.

There are now no less than 200 patients who have made profession of Christian faith; they are a praying, studying, sharing, worshipping, but at the same time very human and fallible, community. And when we had talked together of the treasures of the Gospel they told me that one of their cherished hopes was to build some day a really worthy House of God, in Chinese style, set gloriously on a spur of the hills, so that every passing seafarer might look upon this lighthouse of the Spirit.

A few days later I was in Formosa. Waiting at the airport for us was Dr. G. Gushue-Taylor, together with Formosan and Chinese friends. Dr. Gushue-Taylor was back in the island engaging, as it proved, in his last enterprise of Christian fellowship. He had retired many years before to Canada after his long missionary service. During that service he had established in 1932 the Happy Mount Leprosy Colony, seventeen miles outside Taipeh, and to which he took us. When he established this colony he desired to express the Christian approach to the need of the leprosy sufferer, rather than the official and purely secular one. And so he built a colony which provided a Christian all-round concern, and a place for Christian worship. I was interested in the quotation from John Wesley which in bold Chinese characters was inscribed on the pulpit, " Fear no one but God. Be ashamed of nothing but sin." Dr. Gushue-Taylor had also seen the immense need to bring to the Government Leprosarium outside Taipeh, and at that time under the direction of the Japanese, the Hope of the Gospel, and a place of Christian worship. So he worked, with inflexible determination, to secure consent and then funds for the provision of a church building. World War II intervened before he was able to build. When at last personal circumstances provided opportunity for him to return to Formosa. Dr. Gushue-Taylor, now a man of seventy, went back to accomplish his aim. He found a land far different from the one he had left behind. Liberation from the Japanese had brought strange consequences; and also the war within China itself, leading to the Nationalist Government from the mainland making its headquarters in Formosa. He found the Government Leprosarium a melancholy place. Suicides among the patients were not infrequent. The place was incredibly overstaffed, but quite inadequately supplied with drugs, while children of patients abounded in the institution, running grave risks of infecttion. Other missionaries, and notably Mrs. Dickson, endeavoured to meet this need, and I pay tribute to their tenacity of purpose amid most dispiriting conditions. Dr. Gushue-Taylor knew that his task was to go ahead, swiftly and confidently, with the delayed church building. And when we visited the leprosarium and saw the sad situation of some 750 men patients (including 200 soldiers) and 150 women it was easy to see how great was the value of Dr. Gushue-Taylor's determination and how true his insight. The institution is called Lo San, Happy Home, but it was far from that; and the new church building was itself the one rallying point of hope. That indeed was its name—The Church of Holy Hope. Living night and day in the vestry room at the back of the church, so as to be on the spot, was a German Sister, Sister Alma, whom we met there. She was one of the evacuee missionaries from the Chinese mainland, and in simplicity and trust accepted her new conditions as God's opportunity for her. There in the church gathered the Christian believers among the patients to worship and find refreshment and new courage. And from there they took the influence of their faith back to their fellow-patients in the buildings up on the hillside, and which hid so much suffering and misery.

Three months after our visit, Dr. Gushue-Taylor died. The instancy of his action when opportunity came to build the church at the Government Leprosarium showed how well he had understood that " the King's business requireth haste ". He was another of the Apostles of the Gospel who, finishing the course with unslackened pace, kept the faith.

It was interesting to reflect upon the nature of this last concern of Dr. Gushue-Taylor for the people of Formosa at this eventful, uncertain hour of its history, and compare it with the efforts being made upon the island by other people and governments and organizations. We were in Formosa only a short while, but in that time met representatives of numerous bodies, official and unofficial. We saw the coming of some 4,000 Chinese ex-prisoners of war who had elected to come to Formosa from Korea, crowds and fire crackers, and flags hanging from buildings in regimented uniformity, welcoming them. And as we waited at the airport before leaving for Japan we watched the U.S.A. Army Secretary arrive to a salute of nineteen guns, and the playing of the U.S.A. and Chinese Nationalist national anthems, after which he motored away to Taipeh past a colossal statue of Chiang Kai-shek. Activity and movement abounded, and yet it seemed confused and leading to no clear goal of peace. Amid all this stood Dr. Gushue-Taylor, the medical missionary who had done so much for the repair of broken bodies in past years, concentrating his final energies upon the building of a church, The Church of Holy Hope, for broken, dispirited people, doing all that human hands could do to provide the instrument within which God might bring to the souls of men that abiding peace which none might wrest away.

One would like to give many more instances of the vital part the Christian fellowship of believers takes in the life of a Leprosy Home; but I must confine myself to brief quotations from three missionary doctors in Africa, each in charge of a Home, one in Kenya, one in the French Gabon, and the third in Nigeria. They combine to illustrate the parts of preaching and prayer and the sacrament of holy communion in the total religious life and witness.

A letter from the Rev. A. C. Irvine, M.D., from Chogoria in Kenya, written in August, 1954, while the Mau Mau troubles were creating disturbance in that unhappy land, gives a wonderful picture of peace in the Christian faith.

"This evening at 5.15—it was chilly and damp—I went down to the Leprosy Home to take a service and administer the sacrament. The patients came in mostly with warm pullovers, but Mutune was shivering. 'My pullover went for repair,' she said. I sent her for her blanket, but Mutune is so bent, another woman said, 'I'll go.' Before she went she touchingly put a 5-cent piece—her collection—on the table, so as not to drop it from her partly-paralyzed hands.

"Obadia, who is completely blind, was deemed too ill to come, but I said he could come on a stretcher, so four of them fetched him and he lay with one end of the stretcher upon a form. We sang, 'We praise Thee O God,' and 'What a Friend we have in Jesus'. Amos is the best-educated of them and found the places for two of the others. Andana is always sensible, cheerful and helpful. I spoke, after reading I John iv, 10, about personal friendship with the Lord Jesus. Then, after another hymn, the others left and I held the Holy Communion service for those who partake.

" Is there a more moving sight than a blind leper? Obadia cannot feel, so he just opened his mouth to receive the bread and wine."

And away at Lambarene, Dr. Schweitzer gives us a glimpse of his Sunday services, and the difficulties of speaking in language comprehensible to those who know nothing of the Bible. He urges his hearers to have " the will to let Jesus have power in their hearts " and tries to explain " the innermost fact involved in becoming a Christian—namely, the being led captive by Christ."

" The difficulties which have to be overcome are more than compensated for by the permission of writing the words of Scripture on the hearts of men to whom they are sometimes entirely new. When I speak of the difference between the heart that knows no peace and the heart that is full of peace, the most savage of ' mes sauvages ' know what I mean. And when I describe Jesus as He who brings peace with God into the hearts of men and women, they understand Him."

Finally there is Dr. A. B. Macdonald, who after retirement returned again in 1954 to the great Leprosy Settlement at Itu which he founded, in order that he might fill a gap in staffing. This is what he found.

" There is a congregation of about 2,000 every Sunday, old and young, some educated but the majority illiterate, some from our own (the Church of Scotland) and other missions, very many from heathen homes who had not heard the Gospel message before.

" Those desiring membership have to attend the catechumen class for at least a year, and at the same time, if illiterate, are required to attend the adult school for reading in the evenings. It certainly costs something to be a church member, calling for the sacrifice of time, and great patience and perseverance in those long past school age. And there is profound disappointment if,

when they appear before the Session, they are considered
'not ready' for membership.

"Church members help in the organizations of the
Church : the Men's Meeting, the Women's Guild, the
Sunday Schools; and they visit those who are unable to
get about. In every street and hospital ward there are
evening prayers, led by the Church members there. Thus
there are about forty-five meetings for prayer every
night.

"A stranger going from one meeting to another will
see a little company in each street, gathered round a
storm-lantern, and in the hush of the evening he will be
conscious, as a hymn is being sung or prayer offered, that
'surely the Lord is in this place'.

"After Communion there is a very beautiful custom
begun by the people themselves. They escort each newly-
joined member in procession, with the singing of hymns,
to his home, and there gather round his door, and offer
prayer on his behalf, before he enters his home and his
new life."

VI

But there may be question marks shooting up in the
minds of some readers as to whether the vigorous church
life in these Homes is not attributable to the exceptionally
favourable circumstances in which patients find themselves (I exclude the leprosarium called So Lan in Formosa
which I have described) housed, cared for, treated medi-
cally with skill and sympathy, members once again of a
community. How far is their religious faith conditioned
by human friendship? And if that were withdrawn would
faith also fail?

It is not to be denied that Christian friendship is the
best introduction to the Christian Faith. It would be
wholly anomalous if the behaviour of the messenger of

the Faith contradicted his proclamation. The Gospel is commended by deed more than by word. Nevertheless it would be wholly wrong to conclude that the Faith, once embraced, is powerless to sustain loyalty and devotion when the support of human aids fails. On the contrary, it has proved again and again to be the one unshakeable assurance, enabling men in acute and prolonged adversity to be saved by hope.

There were occasions on this recent tour when I saw the shining lamp of faith burning with startling brightness in dark situations. In Karachi and Calcutta I found crippled victims of leprosy, reduced to roadside begging, whose consolation and courage and cheerfulness were rooted in the Eternal Hope. It was strangely moving, by what appeared to be the merest chance, to meet a small group of Christian beggars with leprosy at Karachi when our steamer called briefly at that port. The Mission had no work there; it was hot; and we decided not to go ashore. But an hour and a half before we were due to sail in the evening my wife and I walked down the gangway with the intention of stretching our legs on the quayside. And at that moment some friends were returning to the ship, and they introduced us to their hostesses for the day who had brought them back.

"Oh, Mr. Miller," said one. "How strange! I had been meaning to write to you; have you time to come and see a little group of Indian Christians with leprosy whom we discovered when visiting a refugee slum?"

So we crowded into a "baby" Austin, and as darkness fell drove into Karachi. As we moved along the MacLeod Road, Miss Laugesen told me of how some Indian patients at the Karachi municipal leprosy institution had been discharged after Partition to make room for Pakistani and contagious cases. They were crippled and unable to return to India and to the Madras State from which they had wandered years ago—itself a commentary on the inadequacy of the institutions in Madras to cope with the large problem there. So they settled with a small group of beggars on a waste piece of land in the heart of the city, which was soon to become crowded with refugees. " They were so glad to see us as fellow-Christians, and we visit them occasionally. Can you advise us?"

We pulled up, and walked behind the buildings of the main road to a huddle of refugee huts. We were led by devious alleyways, and came to a very narrow passage. It was now dark. " We're here," said Miss Laugesen. She led the way, and we followed single file. " This is their little chapel," she said, turning round. On the left there was a low, open doorway. I stooped and looked in. It was no bigger than a cell, about seven feet by five feet, with matting walls, and a very low-pitched roof. Opposite the doorway was a rough table; and on it a tiny open-wick lamp, alight. And beside it a Bible. All the rest was in deep shadow.

In a moment the little group had emerged from their shacks, where the evening meal was cooking at the end of their day of begging; and since Tamil or Telegu was their language, we conversed through the *lingua franca* of Hindustani. Our visit was a complete surprise; and yet there after sundown was that open little chapel, and the lit lamp, and the open Bible for the evening worship. The chapel had been built by them, entirely unaided. " They *never* ask us for personal help," said Miss Laugesen. " Their only request ever has been that if we could help them with some longer timber they could raise the roof, and we might then get in the chapel without crouching down." " Can I do anything for you?" I asked this gallant group. " Sahib, we can't get Tamil and Telegu Bibles and hymn books here. Do you think . . . ?" " Why of course." (And a little later patients in our Homes at Vizianagram and Vadathorasalur gladly collected to send them these books as a Christmas offering.) As we returned to the road two of the younger men came to see us off in the car. " Your names?" I asked. " Mine's John," said one. And, " Mine's Stephen," said the other. John and Stephen. Two precious names in the list of Christian disciples and martyrs. And there, on that hot night in a Muslim city, I stood with other disciples who knew suffering, but also in spite of it all the joy of the Lord. Their faith most certainly did not depend on worldly gain.

It was the same at Calcutta, where the dear old " Padre Babu," John Fernandez, took us to a *busti*, or group of primitive dwellings, where about one hundred beggars with leprosy lived, of whom a number are Christians. For over thirty years Mr. Fernandez has made these and other beggars with leprosy his special care; and the affection and respect in which they hold him shows how great is his influence over them. Those whom we met, variously deformed by leprosy, had forfeited their morning's takings to greet us, for they had been forewarned of our coming, and they even had got some coloured paper and made festoons to welcome us, not as visitors who might offer them bounty, for there was no thought of that. We were simply friends in the Faith, and to be received as such. They were a noisy, chattering, cheerful, excited crowd, and to them the message of eternal hope had a deeper meaning than for those wrapped round with luxury and wealth.

But it was in Korea that we found the fairest flowering of faith, under conditions of adversity. We went there in the middle of cold winter, but if our bodies froze our hearts warmed! The night immediately before we left Tokyo was reported to be the coldest since the war; and snow was piled up in orderly heaps by the roadsides as our luxury taxicab took us out to the airport. It was a very different car which took us from the airport outside Pusan into that devastated city—an almost springless jeep rattling over pitted, stony roads, and very imperfectly protected from the freezing air and the mounting dust. It was bewildering to see the crowds of improvised shacks made by refugees, the great area of devastation in the heart of the city caused by fires, the tough and sturdy people moving about their business, the endless processions of military vehicles careering this way and that, rattling and banging over the unrepaired highways, the complete lack of colour on buildings which had not been painted for many years, the absence of every sign of a people at ease.

Our host was the Rev. George Anderson of the Australian Presbyterian Mission. It was in response to his strong request that we made the journey. The senior member of his depleted Mission, and a wise and saintly man, he was able to see how great the need was to re-establish leprosy work, but was quite unable to add to his own personal responsibilities. Years ago The Mission to Lepers provided the funds for the building and maintenance of a very successful Leprosy Home at Pusan which began its work shortly before the first world war. Under the devoted leadership of the Rev. James Noble Mackenzie it had engaged in a magnificent work right up to 1941, when the Japanese commandeered the site, which occupied a military strategic position above the harbour, and destroyed the buildings. All possibility of the Mission rendering further help at some other site was denied through the outbreak of hostilities between Japan and the Allies at the end of that year. Silence fell upon the situation, and the fate of the patients, of whom there were some 600, could only be conjectured. Among them many had become Christians, and there was a very active self-propagating and self-supporting Church in the Colony. The motto of Korean missionary work from the beginning that every convert should be a missionary was well observed. Now that a Dispersion had been forced on the patients, what would they do?

Many of them were sent to a wooded valley leading down to the sea, where there were some rough barrack buildings and where a pittance of rice was provided. Others went off on their own into the country, and on bare, uncultivated hillsides became settlers and did what they could to make the land productive. It is not at all clear to me how they survived. It is probable that some sort of public grant of rice was given them, but little if anything else. The world was at war, and the care of sufferers from leprosy was a last, and not a first, concern. No longer was help forthcoming from friends of The Mission to Lepers in far parts of the world. No longer could these needy folk communicate with them, as they had done before through messages which they gave to visitors. There is a poignancy today in looking back on records of the time when the Pusan Home flourished. I found a translation of a welcome address to the Mission's medical adviser in the Far East.

" Wholly unexpectedly, from The Mission to Lepers money was sent and these Homes were built, and from all sides lepers came, were received, and, through being clothed, fed, and given good medicine, where formerly every year scores died of the disease, now there is every appearance that we are getting stronger; we are less loathsome to look upon, and before us there is hope in life. For these great blessings, the gratitude we feel toward God and The Mission to Lepers is too great for our lips to express. For the hope of eternal life for our souls which we have received through the death of our Lord Jesus Christ on the Cross, and for our diseased bodies being thus cared for so that we enjoy so much peace and happiness, we give thanks, and thanks again.

" Cared for with grace such as that which cares for fatherless children and rescues drowning men, our gladness and thankfulness cause tears of gratitude to come to our eyes, and for this and the unmeasurable happiness of our souls we give thanks and glory to God. Until this world passes away, please continue to save lepers.

"Are all the believing brethren of your home-country church in peace? Are all The Missions to Lepers' Committee members in peace? Are your own wife and family in peace? In spite of storms at sea and tiredness in travelling, are you also in peace?

"All the inmates of the Pusan Leper Asylum unite in this letter of welcome."

But what of the Faith now? And the spirit of thankfulness?

It was a day of biting winds when we travelled out to one of the countryside groups. We journeyed by jeep some twenty miles between snow-sprinkled hills, passing tiny Manchurian ponies drawing carts, and men with great loads on their backs, and hundreds of army lorries. Then we walked another mile or so across terraced fields, some flooded and frozen, and climbed to a hamlet of cottages on the slope of the hill. Here some eighty men and women with leprosy, and twenty children, lived. Our visit was expected, and we were greeted by a group of men who took us straight to the church, where all the others were waiting. It was a plain, rough building, made from stone which the Christians had hewn from the hillside, and bound with mud. The places for windows were covered with torn khaki-green cloth. We passed through the open doorway into semi-darkness. Seated on the ground, some on cardboard strips from army cartons, and some on straw mats, was a crowded company of praying people. They did not stir on our arrival but continued at audible prayer. We were asked to sit down on a couple of packing-cases facing the congregation. There was a table with a coarse blanket on it, a bell, and a Bible. After a minute a visiting Korean pastor struck the bell, the praying ceased, and the bowed heads were raised. Eyes turned upon us. We looked into the shadowed and marred faces of these faithful people. Then followed a service of song and prayer and reading. During the pastor's prayer the congregation made vocal assent. And when I was called on to speak by interpretation, the company bowed and murmured approval after each passage was translated. I was told that it was Christian leaders from among patients at the old Pusan Home who had knit together into a community this group which would have been pathetic if it had not been so heroic. They told those who joined them of their Christian faith and hope in a God Who would certainly vindicate Himself, of Christ victorious through suffering, of an eternal reward for those who endured to the last. Obviously there was a strong apocalyptic note in their thinking and preaching. This temporal life had given them no substantial, lasting joys. They looked to a life beyond in

143

which God's loving purpose would be fully revealed; and meantime offered Him their sacrifice of praise in this mountain Bethel which they had set up.

There was another day when we travelled in an olive grey-green train, largely occupied with U.N. soldiers, up on the Seoul line as far as Taegu. There the signs of war were not so marked and the large Leprosy Home with 1,000 patients, now financed by American Leprosy Missions and built by The Mission to Lepers over forty years ago, still continues to function. It is superintended by American Presbyterians; there is a very large membership of the church, and its band welcomed us with resounding music. From Taegu we motored on to a new leprosy colony set gloriously amid remote hills and being largely developed by the patients themselves, with government help. Here again a Christian group of patients had shown extraordinary enterprise and enthusiasm, making the building of a temporary church a priority obligation. Because they intend building a better one later they did not nail the timber they had secured from the woods, but tied it together, so that narrow lines of sunlight came pouring in through the gaps between the planks. At one end the wall was only sackcloth. On the bare floor there was a pulpit and, surprisingly, a harmonium. At this Ai Sang Won, as it is called—Love Life Garden—there was a most vigorous central emphasis on a life rooted in eternity, and discovered in Christ.

But it was of the valley that leads to the sea that I have the most vivid recollection, so challenging and overwhelming was the experience which was ours when Mr. Anderson took us there on a Sunday morning. We made our way down between stubby pine trees and cottages which in many cases had roofs made from flattened-out salmon and bully beef tins passed on by army canteens. We came to a level strip of land behind a narrow beach upon which the waves pounded. There was a long row of children, over 200 of them, standing there in the biting wind at the close of their Sunday school, waiting with their teachers—all patients—to greet us. It was tragic to know that they were living in overcrowded cottages with their parents, and that many of them must have already contracted the disease. After we had smiled at them and moved among them, they ran off and we moved to the crowd of adult settlers who were waiting for us at the one substantial building in the village. This had been a Japanese army storehouse; and the large company of Christian patients who had been exiled here from the old Pusan Home turned it into their place of worship. Outside was a short granite pillar, one that the patients had erected at the old Home in honour of Mr. Mackenzie, and which they uprooted and brought with them. The building was already completely crowded out, and some sat outside in the icy wind, for there were many degrees of frost. Shoes or sandals were removed by those who went inside. Many were woefully marred and crippled by the disease; a number were blind. The window-frames were covered with opaque paper, often torn; and patches of cloth were here and there put up to block open spaces. The rushing wind made the sheets of corrugated iron roof, which were often loose and pierced with holes, shake and clatter. We took our places as we had done at the hillside church. It was desperately moving to look on this tightly-packed company, for the building could only hold about 400 at the most, and as many as possible crowded in. The singing was hearty and in tune. What singers the Korean Christians are! (One evening we heard the

Hallelujah Chorus sung gloriously at a church in the town by college and high school students.) They began with the Korean version of " Holy, Holy, Holy ", and ended with " Jesus, keep me near the Cross ", and after the benediction sang " The Lord bless thee and keep thee . . ." before dispersing. A choir of the less advanced cases sang an anthem. Elders took part in prayer and Bible reading. One old man, with large record book, took note of every stage of the proceedings. When the time came for the collection, bags on long poles were passed along the tight rows. Where the money came from was a mystery to me until I heard that some went out to beg in the town; others had relatives who in spite of their own hardships forwarded to them what they could spare; others saved something from their small ration of rice. To give to God's work was a primary call, however ragged, ill-shod, ill-housed, ill-fed they were themselves. There were a few folded bits of paper with special offerings inside and, written in Korean, such explanations as " On my birth-day " or "A late harvest gift ". It was hard to have a right message when the time came for the sermon which I had been invited to give by interpretation. This congregation was saying so much to me, of loyalty, courage, liberality, faith and hope. Here was a people, deep in adversity, who were truly able to say with St. Paul, " Most gladly therefore will I rather glory in my weaknesses, that the power of Christ may rest upon me." In that wild valley one might see most clearly, as a rainbow against a dark sky, the Arch of Eternal Hope.

It is, of course, an immense challenge to men of Christian goodwill throughout the world to bring to these folk, and others in Korea like them, relief in their distress. It is necessary for me to break off from the subject of this chapter to say that in some countries today, where governments are now providing proper Homes and medical treatment for in-patients and also treatment for those still living in their villages, the part of the Christian mission is to bring words of spiritual comfort and illumination; but in South Korea the situation is reversed. The sufferers from leprosy are themselves the messengers of the Gospel to others, the builders of the Arch of Eternal Hope; but they are, in and around Pusan particularly, most desperately in need of proper medical care, and decent housing, and friendship. They need the other arches of the Bridge of Compassion. And for the children, exposed to such grave risks, the challenge is even greater. When I found that none, adult or child, in that valley of 1,500 people was receiving the sulphone drugs, and that the relief agencies spoke of their helplessness to secure them through official channels, our Mission immediately found a way of getting supplies in regularly, month by month. But in many cases there are not the trained people to administer treatment wisely. It can only be said here that the Mission is endeavouring to recruit a trained missionary team, and to make provision for the saving of the smaller children by establishing a separate children's crèche and kindergarten, where they can live until they can be passed on to other agencies caring for older destitute children. As I write this page, both Dr. Cochrane and Dr. Fraser, of whom I have written, are due within a month to make visits to help forward practical action. The amount of leprosy in South Korea is far too great for any private organization to cope with; the challenge is rather to do something provocative, to do it in the right way, and to encourage by co-operative action all who on the spot can directly engage in so great a task.

A Bridge of Compassion

I have left, for the last three pages of this book, room to refer again to " The Bridge Beyond ", which is all of God's building. It only remains for me, in this chapter, to say a final word about the building of that bridge of compassion about which the main part of the book tells. We have seen a little of what loving service of physical need does, and what the extended hand of human friendship achieves, and the proclamation of the Gospel of Hope and the organization of Christian fellowships. This work builds a bridge that becomes a sure highway over the waters of trouble. And in opening up this highway for a peculiarly needy people it also declares that compassion is the great constructive, healing, and liberating energy which God puts into a man's heart for him to use for the redemption of every sphere of life.

There is still very much that remains to be done in this special field of activity which we have been considering. If there is now a broad network of activity, in much of which The Mission to Lepers is privileged to have a share, it is a thin one with gaps which are far too broad. There is, for instance, still no work in Nepal, now open to foreign missions. That is a land in which there is much leprosy, as the past has made clear by the numbers who have crossed to India to find refuge at mission Homes such as those at Chandag Heights and Almora. The same is true of Bhutan and Tibet. And there are great areas of unmet need in countries where already work has been established, but which is altogether inadequate. Pioneer work is also called for in parts of Africa not yet helped at all. And to meet this need there is especially a call for dedicated, skilled hands and trained, active minds to give effect to the desires of the loving heart, and the gifts of the opened purse. New times, new discoveries need new approaches, new techniques. But basically the task remains the same, to respond to the cry of those who are like the man who called out to the Lord Jesus Christ, " Lord, if thou wilt, thou canst make me clean "; and to obey the command of that same Lord to His disciples, "As ye go, preach, saying, The Kingdom of heaven is at hand. Heal the sick, cleanse the lepers . . ."

THE ARCHES OF THE YEARS

I

Five and a half years have passed since the previous chapters were written. Now, as I read them again, I am able to rejoice over many happy sequels to much that has been recorded. And looking forward to the future, the horizon is shot with light. To the other arches of the bridge must be added the arches of the years. In Tennyson's *Ulysses* the old voyager, returned after his adventures, muses as he looks westward from his craggy home, and sees past and future bound inextricably together as the pillar of a bridge supports the arches on either side of it.

> "I am a part of all that I have met.
> Yet all experience is an arch wherethro'
> Gleams that untravell'd world, whose margin
> fades
> For ever and for ever when I move.
> . . . my purpose holds
> To sail beyond the sunset."

So it is that in the realm of leprosy work events of the last few years are bound to all that has gone before, and are equally linked to "that untravell'd world" which lies beyond the sunset.

I shall only make reference to a few of the developments of the last five years. In the final paragraph of the last chapter appears the sentence "There is, for instance, still no work in Nepal." That is no longer true. With the opening of Nepal to acceptable Christian Missions who would engage in medical and educational work, our Mission, in the autumn of 1955, sent in a small but representative Commission to investigate need, assess opportunity, and suggest lines of action. It had no difficulty in finding the need. Already there had been evidence of it by the fact that numbers of Nepalis with leprosy made arduous journeys across mountainous country to Mission leprosy centres at Chandag Heights, Kalimpong, and even to the more remote Subathu, all in the India hills; and they had also travelled down to Homes in the plains in Uttar Pradesh, Bihar, and West Bengal. The Commission made a journey from Kathmandu to a concentration of nearly five hundred compulsorily segregated sufferers. The buildings were gloomy, and though the inmates received adequate food there was a sad lack of personal attention. Here, year after year, men and women lived together, and bore children who grew up in the asylum. Some youths had never known the outside world; and having contracted the disease within the precincts of the institution had no prospect of any life beyond it. "It was terrible to see such neglected men, women and children amidst such majestic hills and luscious rice fields." There were also four Government sponsored out-patient clinics in the Kathmandu valley, but the modern sulphone treatment had still not been introduced, ten years or so after its inception elsewhere. Further west another concentration of leprosy victims was found. They were courageously cheerful; but no constructive work was being engaged in to bring them hope.

The Commission strongly urged that the challenge of such need be heeded by the Mission. Certain lines of action were recommended, and because of the mountainous nature of the country and the absence of roads it was realised that there could be no immediate establishment of an extensive network of out-patient clinics, except in the Kathmandu valley. The first requirement was to build a residential sanatorium, with modern medical facilities, where patients would be honoured as people, and which would also become a training centre for Nepali workers, and the hub of the Mission's activities.

But where and how should this be built? Government's goodwill and help over the provision of a site were essential. And so Dr. P. J. Chandy (whom we have met already at Faizabad, see pages 79-85) gladly went to Kathmandu as the Mission's envoy and negotiator. With patience, vision, and tact, he steadily built up confidence in Government circles; he established cordial relations with the United Mission to Nepal; he made friends among the exalted and the humble; he engaged in a small amount of out-patient work, using the newest drugs, and he began his hunt for a site which would be at once suitable and obtainable. It was that combination which for months proved elusive. Any spare land was either devoted to the gods, or was inaccessible, or had other impossible objections. Then, late one afternoon, after a day of fruitless journeyings, Dr. Chandy turned aside from the rough road leading from Kathmandu to India, just where the valley begins to be enclosed by steep hills, and found himself in a secluded woodland area, with a running stream at its foot. He had the immediate feeling that this was God's place for the Mission. And so it has proved. The Prime Minister himself had charge of the Ministry of Foreign Affairs, with which our Mission at headquarters was negotiating over terms of entry. Dr. Chandy, after preliminary enquiries over the site, took his request in person to the Prime Minister. And the result was that, for a nominal rent of Rs. 5 a year (seven shillings and sixpence) a site of over forty acres was allotted to the Mission in December 1957. The area was locally known as "Bhangaban"—The Broken Forest. What might it become in the future?

It was just over a year after the agreement had been signed that my wife and I made the short and easy flight from India into Nepal. The Mission had meanwhile come into actual occupation of the site, and the ground-breaking ceremony had taken place two months before our arrival. It was not surprising that the message the Council sent for that occasion was Isaiah 44, 23: "Sing, O ye heavens, for the Lord hath done it . . . Break forth into singing, ye mountains, O forest, and every tree therein. . . ." "Bhangaban"—the Broken Forest—was no longer to be an adequate name; in faith it has been re-named "Anandaban"—the Forest of Joy.

We walked up into the woods through the recently made approach road; looked at the blueprint plans on their respective sites for hospital, cottages, and staff houses; climbed to the 6,000 ft. summit above to look away to the magnificent stretch of mighty Himalayan peaks beyond the Kathmandu valley; watched Dr. Pedley giving treatment to a few leprosy outpatients at the temporary dispensary; descended to the stream far below, from which water was to be lifted by hydram and pump. "Break forth into singing ye mountains, O forest, and every tree therein."

Now, as I write, the building work proceeds, with

all the difficulties of starting from absolute scratch. And news has recently come of the admission, on June 24th, 1960, of the first resident patients, one of whom had journeyed three weeks over the mountains, with ulcerated feet. It is a far cry to the opening in 1884 of the Mission's Home at Chandag Heights on the Indian side of the Nepal border, and the arrival there of Nepali victims of the disease, "some of them to escape being buried alive", * as the record I have just looked up states. The arches of the years reach back and forward, bound by each day's labour and prayer, and we now look forward to the development of this new and most significant work in the heart of Nepal, and give thanks for its beginning.

II

A more rapid development has been in South Korea. I have in the last chapter written of the visit I made early in 1954, and of the contrast, so moving, between the strong Christian faith of many leprosy sufferers there, and the lack of proper medical attention and personal friendship. The challenge cried out for the Mission to go in to engage in some constructive work, something which would bring the breath of hope, and which would show, by our identification with the people of South Korea at one point of their great need, our desire to lift a little of the burden of their suffering.

I visited South Korea again in the autumn of 1958. On this occasion I flew in a comfortable 'plane from Hong Kong to Seoul, with one brief stop at Taiwan where, instead of the usual tea, we were served with

* *Lepers*, by John Jackson, 1906, p. 38. Published by The Mission to Lepers. (Out of print.)

154

slices of pineapple. We passed along the irregular Korean coast line, fringed with lace-like surf, the brown land with a patch-work quilt of gold and green fields upon it. I was grateful that now I would be met by the first of our Mission's small team, and that I would be confronted not only with need but also some evidence of the Mission's response to that need. And when I passed out of the warm 'plane into the keen, sweet air of a late October evening, there was Mr. Lloyd waving to me from beyond the barrier and also, as a gesture of that Korean courtesy with which I was soon to become so familiar, a representative of the Health Department, Dr. Yun.

When the Council of the Mission determined that it must do something, however small, the first need was to find a man young enough to have energy and imagination, old enough to face with equanimity whatever situation of emergency or difficulty might arise, and Christian enough to "labour and not to look for any reward" save that of knowing he was doing God's Will. On the Mission's Home staff was an ex-missionary, the Rev. C. M. Lloyd, who joined us after the second world war, when he was a Chaplain in Burma, and where he first came into touch with the Mission's Home at Moulmein.* When he heard of the need, he and Mrs. Lloyd at once offered to go out. "We want to be stretched," he said, "while we have strength." There was no difficulty in providing the stretching exercise! And in the spring of 1956 Mr. and Mrs. Lloyd, together with the first nursing sister, Miss Grace Bennett, landed at Pusan with their luggage, their faith, and a general commission to be helpful where possible to existing groups of

* See *Red Earth and Summer Lilies,* p. 164.

unshepherded leprosy victims, to endeavour to establish the nucleus of a Korean team, while the Mission made preparations to send out a doctor and a further nurse from England, and to feel their way in the establishment of pioneer village treatment and teaching work.

In this last object there was not unnaturally a certain amount of opposition to be faced; it ran counter to Government's policy of compulsory segregation. But very soon there was a remarkable change of attitude. Both at the local and at the top administrative level goodwill and even co-operation was secured. Mr. Lloyd found that the area in greatest need was that around Taegu, which was even called "Mudongie-Do" or Leper Land. So the little team moved there; and soon a room in this village, or an abandoned military building outside that one, was made available, and simple clinics began to be established. Within four years thirteen such clinics were in action, radiating from Taegu, and engaging in a work of such significance that Government's own policy began to change. Medical help was also given at the National Leprosarium at points where there was special need—over dressings, care of the eyes, the provision of artificial legs. And recently the Medical College and Hospital at Taegu has asked the Mission to establish a small centre there for leprosy patients requiring temporary hospital care, and this has been done. This marks a radical change in attitude, and is of the greatest encouragement.

But there is still much prejudice to overcome, in some parts more than in others. A sharp reminder of this was in the murder of twenty-five desperate leprosy victims on August 28th, 1957, who had tried to settle on some unoccupied land on Bito Island, just off the mainland,

Dr. Pedley among the children at the Government Asylum in the Kathmandu Valley.   See page 151

NEPAL

Planning the position of buildings at the site for the Mission's leprosy sanatorium at Bhangaban. See pages 152-154

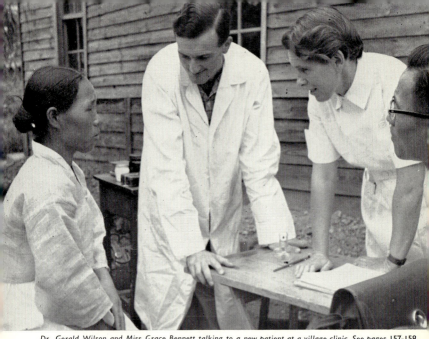

Dr. Gerald Wilson and Miss Grace Bennett talking to a new patient at a village clinic. See pages 157-158

KOREA

Patients at work on the Church extension at Sang Ae Won. See pages 160-161

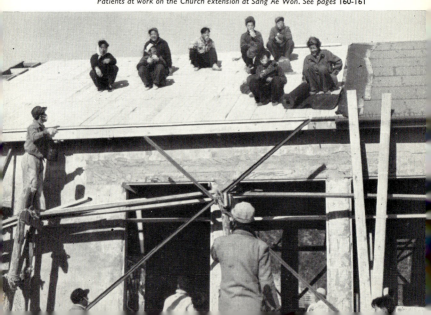

after their application to Government for an allotment of land had been rejected. The villagers from another part of the island made an organised attack on them, leaving twenty-five killed and fifty-six injured. The Korean Press was aroused, and called for a new approach to the whole problem. And it is certain that Government is now, amid many other problems, doing much more that is both humane and enlightened. At the great island segregation centre of Sorok-Do, with over five thousand patients, Mr. Lloyd found when he visited it for the first time only one very elderly doctor; four years later there were eight, supported by a good staff. It was a surprise one day for Mr. Lloyd to be called by Government to receive an address in Korean and in English, bearing the signature and seal of the Minister of Health, and ceremoniously wrapped up in blue silk and red ribbon. It expressed the thanks of Government for what The Mission to Lepers, through its team in Korea, was doing and which had "brought about the betterment and improvement of leprosy control in this country". The address concluded with a passage commending "services which have warmed the hearts and raised the spirits of the people of Korea".

While I was in Korea I visited some of the clinics at which our little team worked. We would crowd into a sturdy Land Rover, Mr. Lloyd and Miss Bennett, Mrs. Pak the Bible woman, another Mrs. Pak the nurse, Mr. Kim the laboratory technician, Mr. Yong the interpreter, and Shinsi the cheery driver. In the lovely morning light we would drive out from Taegu, soon leaving behind metalled roads and thereafter creating great whirls of dark dust, however discreetly we tried to pass pedestrians. "Hello, O.K.," the children cried to us gaily, a reminder of the contact they have had with U.N. troops from the U.S.A.

When we reached a point where a clinic was to be held there would already be a few waiting patients, the older men sometimes with nanny-goat beards and long witch-like hats. Younger men usually had some item of army attire upon them, a discarded tunic, or a webbing belt, or slim American cut trousers. The women always wore their national dress, voluminous skirts, often of black velvet, and white blouses, with their shining black hair parted in the middle and tightly plaited behind. Always I noticed, whatever the physical condition of the patient, a courteous and smiling approach. There was a quite extraordinary quiet, and attentive reverence, during the short devotional period; and then, with all the gear set out, the routine of the day's work began. One would have charge of the records, another of dressings, another (Miss Bennett, acting perforce as doctor until the arrival of a "real" one) of examination and prescription, another of dispensing and any microscopic tests. A little box for any "Thank You" gift was at the foot of Miss Bennett's table, and I noticed that nearly all gave their mite. Indeed, I saw one woman patient struggling up from the road to the somewhat elevated site at Yongchun with a sizeable wooden box clasped between her arms. Out of breath and with a dump she set it at Miss Bennett's feet, and gave her a charming smile. "Apples from our trees, Lady; and God bless you for your goodness." Later we all enjoyed some of the generous supply of this gift of gratitude.

It was at Yongchun also that we visited two contrasting sites. One was down by a river bed, dry for most of the year. Here a group of socially unwanted leprosy sufferers had built slum shacks, going out on begging expeditions to neighbouring villages. When I visited the site only one shack was left occupied; the others were destroyed. A woman was there and a couple of children. "My man is over at the new site, building there; I'll be joining him soon," she said.

The "new site" was a patch of land half a mile away, well above the high-water level of the river when in flood. Mr. Lloyd had helped secure it, and here we found a group of some forty men and women furiously busy making mud bricks, sawing wooden doors, putting up walls and so erecting a reasonably neat little village before the winter set in. Mr. Lloyd had told me I would meet at the site a Korean gentleman whom he had interested, and who had helped in securing the site; I met him and his son, and also another Korean who was ready to negotiate with us for a field nearby which we bought there and then for the patients, so that they might have their own farmland, even if inadequate in size fully to support them. Relief work must go hand in hand with the work of rehabilitation, and there can be no hard and fast line, in any situation of need, between "charity" and constructive effort. The patients, though some were woefully disfigured, were men and women with a new hope; and what was most moving of all was to see, in the corner of this little hamlet-in-the-making, an ex-army patched tent, with a rather unerect wooden cross surmounting it. "Right from the beginning the Christians have set aside a place for their worship and their study of the Word of God," I was told. On that crisp early November morning I saw on a bare hillside, with the flatter country stretching out before me and glittering in the sunlight, a little company of those who give to life a glorious quality of faith and courage, in the face of great material adversity, and who have come to their victory through the love of friends in far-away lands, who have known that they must take their part in fulfilling the command to "bear ye one another's burdens, and so fulfil the law of Christ".

The Mission has, of course, a special ministry to engage in among those who are Christian, and have found in the Faith their spiritual succour and deliverance. On pages 144-146 I have told of our visit to the Christian congregation down in the valley by the sea outside Pusan, and of their quite miraculous devotion. At that time, when I asked their leaders if there was anything the Mission could do in a practical way, they asked for nothing for themselves, but said "Help us to build a worthy House of God". I was able to negotiate with the U.N. General in charge at Pusan for some material as I sat in his cosily heated and modernly lighted Nissen hut. "Well," he said—the armistice had recently been signed—"if they won't let us fight in the north we'd better make friends in the south." Supplies of material no longer required for military purposes were generously given; and when Mr. Lloyd first visited Sang Ae Won the new church had been completed. But almost immediately it proved too small for the large congregation, and further help was sent to enable an extension to be made. This is what Mr. Lloyd wrote at the end of 1956 :—

"A couple of days before Christmas we received a message from the Pastor to the effect that they would not be able to have their service on Christmas morning, as the alterations to their church were not complete,

160

but they expected to get things ready for a service on the 26th. We carried out our original idea and visited them on Christmas morning. We made our way up the hill to the church, and what a hive of industry we found. With great enthusiasm many of the patients were working to complete their church building, some on the roof, some on window frames, some on the floor. There appeared to be so much to be finished that we could not see how the building could possibly be ready for a service on the 26th, but they assured us that it would be.

"We went again to Sang Ae Won on the morning of the 26th and to our amazement we found the church finished and the people assembled for Christmas service. The church was packed and we were very glad indeed that The Mission to Lepers had made it possible for them to put this work in hand, as during the winter months it has certainly been very hard for those who have had to sit outside the church because of lack of space inside."

Altogether, in the last five years, nine churches have been built in Korea, with the Mission's encouragement and help; pastoral care is provided at the National Leprosarium north of Taegu, and in various ways Christian fellowship has been established.

So the work goes forward. A young missionary doctor and a second nurse are now in Korea learning the language and gaining experience. A site has been secured for the Mission's centre, both for the residence of staff and for medical purposes. The network of out-patient clinics cannot continue to be the rim of a wheel without any hub on which to revolve. There is laboratory work to be engaged in, and hospital accommodation for those requiring to come in for some orthopaedic operation, or for special observation because of obscure symptoms.

The passing of the years has already abundantly justified the action taken. If it were possible to do nothing more, the venture would already have justified itself, setting in motion new methods, arousing new hope, creating new bonds of friendship. But we believe that more will be done, and that other victories of the Gospel of Christ's compassion will be achieved.

III

In the earlier pages of this book the references to Africa are few, because I wrote especially of those pieces of leprosy work with which I was personally acquainted. Only on pages 33-34, 48-49, 108-114 and 134-136 are there references to Africa stations. But between December, 1955, and March, 1956, my wife and I visited a considerable amount of the work with which The Mission to Lepers is linked in Nigeria, the Congo, Ruanda-Urundi, Uganda, Tanganyika and Ethiopia. Leprosy work in Africa, except in the extreme south, was for the most part off to a later start than in Asia. When it did begin in territories of a colonial status it was sometimes the case that Governments were glad to use the enterprise, sympathy and experience of missionaries, while they supplied the basic funds. In other cases missionaries were the ones to launch out in faith while Government remained passive, our Mission encouraging these pioneers by the supply of funds. Frequently these ventures of faith became so significant and hopeful that Governments offered increasingly substantial help, until they became important centres of anti-leprosy campaigns. So our Mission's part through the years has differed quite considerably from that which it was called on to fufil in Asia. Sometimes it was to "prime the pump", sometimes to provide for the healthy children, or staff houses, frequently to make provision for church buildings or for medical equipment; and most of all to provide annual grants-in-aid which made it possible for the local Missions and missionaries to engage in a fuller, more all-round work than would have been possible on the bare bones of grants received by Government, and also to maintain freedom from Government direction. Altogether in Africa the Mission now supports 49 stations in 16 countries, and it has been of vast encouragement to see how through the years, and particularly the last thirty, the co-operation of supporters, Missions and missionaries, Governments, and the people themselves, have enabled great progress to be made, though there are still backward areas where pioneer work needs to be engaged in.

Our visit to the countries I have just mentioned was made at an exciting time. Some were passing through a rapid process of change from colonial to self-governing or independent status. Together with the political changes were the advances in medical knowledge, to be appropriated and used without delay. There were also rapid changes in social and religious habits and convictions. An amusing commentary on the times was in the names of the crowded buses we passed as we were motored from place to place in Nigeria. Blazoned over the driving seat were such titles as "Wake Up in Time" or "The Greater Tomorrow", or "No Swet, No Sweet". A less stirring, more cautionary name given to one bus was "Take It Easy, Joe"! I thought it good advice when I saw the blithely reckless progress of some drivers!

To add to our own swift movement was the making

of "movies" by my wife. As a result, many thousands of friends, in far separated lands, have been enabled to see in two films the swiftly passing scene, the colour and form, the hope and pathos, the faith and hard work, which make up the many-angled activities of missionary leprosy work.*

I am unable, for lack of space, to write of what we saw in Northern Nigeria, and must confine myself to four projects further south, one a young one, the other three being enterprises which have spanned some thirty years of time's arches.

In the Southern Ogoja area the Church of Scotland has, in the last decade, undertaken a campaign, at Government's request, and with the financial partnership of The Mission to Lepers, to fight leprosy in this relatively populous area. At the central settlement at Uburu we were present at the dedication of the new hospital block. In the large mud and palm church a notable Nigerian Christian doctor, Sir Francis Ibiam, preached the sermon before we walked in procession with the patients to the new building. The next day Dr. Alistair MacDonald and I set off to see some of the many leprosy clinics and villages which have been established, and where now over three thousand patients are being efficiently treated. I had left the Muslim country of the north behind and was now among people emerging from a primitive animism, to whom the Gospel conception of God, and its declaration and incarnation in Jesus Christ, comes as a torch of light brought into a gloomy cavern. After a long journey, in which our car

* *Song of Deliverance.* Sound/Colour. 35 mins.; 16 mm., 16 frames/sec.

I Have Set My Bow. Sound/Colour. 35 mins.; 16 mm., 16 frames/sec.

twice had to be ferried across rivers, and during which we made calls at several clinics and villages supervised or staffed by trained ex-patients, we arrived at Mbembe to be welcomed by nearly seven hundred patients in a leprosy village begun only three years previously. There was a brilliant full moon, and it was a warm night. But we found a huge bonfire blazing, its warm and leaping flames making the dark faces of the hundreds of assembled patients glisten brightly. Before our business the next day we were to be regaled with an entertainment of the patients' own preparation. Ceremoniously (if uncomfortably) seated near to the scorching bonfire, we watched a series of primitive dances, first the women, wearing palm-leaf skirts, and then the men. The *pièce de resistance* was reserved till last. We were told that as very special visitors we were to be favoured to watch something secret. We were to be allowed to witness the Cannibal Dance! Until quite recent years ritual cannibalism has survived in this rather cut-off area, the victim being slain to be offered to the spirits, and then to be eaten after the sacrificial ritual has been performed. So we watched a wild frenzy of shouting, stamping, jumping, twirling. The group would menacingly draw close to us and then retreat. The bonfire was almost too conveniently near! But at last the dance was over, and we were allowed to motor away between the forest trees, nightjars flying off in front of our headlights. The experience was a reminder that we are in a world where the primitive still survives and is far from being idyllic. At that distant settlement at Mbembe darkness and disease required the enlightenment of science and the services of love. At my side, as I sat looking upon the fantastic scene, were a young Christian doctor from Scotland and a self-effacing bachelor layman—Mr. Robert Lowe of B.L.R.A.—from England, who were there with their skills and the sacrifice of their personal ambitions in order that they might bring the light and the salt of truth and goodness, and so that the healing power of true religion might do its transforming work.

At three of the more famous leprosy settlements established between twenty-five and thirty-five years ago —Itu, Uzuakoli and Oji River—we were able to see something of what happens when a right faith, an adventurous pioneer spirit, and scientific skill combine to meet human need on all fronts. "Pneumo-Psycho-Somatic Medicine" is a relatively new phrase, but it has been practised at these three centres, and in the areas to which the work has reached out, ever since their inception. All along it has been recognised that spirit, mind and body require the physician's care if true and full healing is to be achieved. I wish it were possible to write more of our experiences at these centres. Three occasions must suffice as significant pointers.

It was on the Sunday before Christmas that we journeyed out from the Oji River Settlement, over roads with a surface rather like corrugated iron, to a Harvest Festival service at the leprosy clinic at Achi. This is one of thirty-one which dot the countryside around Oji. They have been established over a number of years, and a quite wonderful fact is that no less than twenty of them now have their church buildings, which have the simple beauty of mud, thatch and unplaned wood for pillars and roof-beams. The Church Missionary Society, through its foreign and national workers, has used its evangelistic opportunity to the full; and it was in a car provided by our Mission to enable these various out-stations to be regularly visited that we travelled.

The patients had prepared for the Festival with enthusiasm. Coloured earth—raw and red ochre—was used to make the half-walls cheerful and pleasant. The pulpit and lectern were of grey mud, touched with white. The lines of seats and the floor were of grey mud, edged with white. The patients, eager to begin their service, moved forward in a rather higgledy-piggledy procession to make their offerings at the foot of the apse. Large enamel bowls (we found the African everywhere wedded to enamel!) contained a stringy white substance which we were told was kassava. Generous bunches of bananas; live cocks and fowls; heaps of coins; palm wine; oranges; and a great number of long yams and the smaller coco yams were all presented, together with a curious assortment of other articles. The congregation contained a number of discharged patients who had returned to make their thank-offering. And in the congregation were the first five patients who, Mr. Savory told us, had come to him in 1947 and said: "We receive treatment for our bodies, but we don't have the medicine of your religion. We want to be taught your book, the Bible". It is a matter for rejoicing that as yet the simple rural Nigerian does not split up his life into fragments. And so it has been that a ministry for body, mind and spirit has, without any departmental division, been crowned with great success.

The following Sunday was Christmas Day, and we had the great happiness of spending it at Uzuakoli as the guests of Dr. and Mrs. Frank Davey. It is no wonder that this Settlement has a far-famed reputation. (I

have referred to it on pages 48-49.) For twenty years
Dr. and Mrs. Davey had led the work; and by religious
devotion, wide vision, splendid courtesy, efficient administration and first-class medical work they had enabled
it to become a centre of "sweetness and light". The
results of the work are the most striking demonstration
of success of which I know in overcoming the leprosy
problem in a particular area. At one time the settlement had 1,500 patients. When we visited it the numbers were down to 550. About 60 clinics were established throughout the district, where at one time 16,000
patients received treatment. Now the numbers were
down to 4,000. Though the settlement is today a
Government one, it not only began as an activity of
Methodist missionaries, but ever since the senior doctor-
ing and nursing staff has been appointed by the Methodist Missionary Society. An all-round work of high
quality has been engaged in which has led the way in
showing that the leprosy problem in a rural community
can be solved, if the scope of effort is made broad
enough, the work done is good enough, and the vision of
what a full life really is is clear enough.

It was good to see so live and beautiful a settlement:
the wide avenues of tall palm trees; the charming staff
chapel opened while we were there; the excellent
laboratory and hospital; the glorious cannas in the terraced garden looking out over savannah-like country;
the cottages and the children's wing; the great church
at the heart of all, where at midnight we met with the
Christian staff and patients and joined in the Communion Service, with Dr. Davey—himself an ordained
minister—and the African pastor conducting the worship. The house of our hosts was full of activity, with

a constant coming and going of guests of different nationalities. In our bedroom were good reproductions of pictures by Vermeer and Van Gogh. But one frame contained another kind of decoration. It was made up of a rather pirate-like, tasseled cap, and a large feather. I asked what it all meant, and found that it was the regalia of a local Order to which Dr. Davey had been ceremoniously admitted: "The Order of Leopard Killers"! As the name implies, it was reserved for those hunters who had brought public benefit by reducing the depredations of these wild animals, and bringing freedom from fear. The Chiefs had come to him and said "You, too, are a huntsman, though you have other game to destroy. You are not a leopard but a leprosy killer. You are ridding us of a great menace; you are bringing us freedom from the fear of a great enemy". A happy and most appropriate gesture. Dr. Davey has recently been made a C.B.E. by Her Majesty the Queen; I am sure that both the honours done him cannot have been better deserved.

And as the previous Sundays were spent at Oji and Uzuakoli, the New Year Sunday was spent at Itu, in Calabar. Near to Itu stands a rugged cairn, a little way up from the road, commemorating the spot where Mary Slessor died. It is on the other side of the town from where the great Itu Leprosy Colony stands, a memorial indeed to the faith and love of Dr. A. B. Macdonald, still with us in Scotland. (I have made brief reference to this work on pages 110-111, and 135-136.)

After a long day's motoring on December 31st, on roads and over tracks as dusty and jolty as the trees on either side were majestic and tranquil, we came at last to the way beside the river which led to the settlement. Below us was the sandbank on which the first hopeful patients had built their shacks thirty-four years ago; before us what had been jungle, now turned into a garden town. At the entrance, in large letters, were the significant words : "In His Name". "You have arrived," we were told, "just in time for the announcement of discharges." A wash and a quick cup of tea, and then we hurried down in the fading light to the open air amphitheatre where nearly two thousand patients were waiting, regaled by the brass band. Our host, the Rev. R. B. Macdonald, spoke to the company, with three translators beside him, including one who turned English into Pidgin English (a recognised language here!). Then came the reading out of names, so fateful for so many. It was exhilarating to see the joy of those who heard their names called. They lifted up their hands to heaven, "Thank you, God, thank you, everyone", and rushed up the steep aisles, as if they were going to depart that minute, though in fact it would be several days before they went. One laddie, wearing only a blue spot shirt, tore it off, waved it like a pennant, and danced naked away. A man, holding an ancient gun in readiness, fired it off when he heard his name. Hand-shaking and boisterous buffeting abounded. The "patient-police" blew their whistles; the band burst into a blare of music when the bandmaster's own name was called. Crackers were let loose. It was a glorious pandemonium of happy excitement. And the disappointed ones showed no signs of envy. Perhaps in six months' time their names would be called. And after all, Itu had almost become home, and a very happy one.

How different was the scene a few hours later! Half

an hour before midnight several hundred of us gathered in the dimly lit great mud and thatch church. It was almost incredibly quiet. There was no trace of the excitement of a few hours ago. We were now in the House of God, and reverence and quiet before Him became our praise. Water-lilies rested on the Holy Table. A short service, in three languages, took place; then silence fell again, a minute or so before midnight. Memories; gratitude; penitence; praise; all were in that silence. Then into it there came the poignant cry of a single bugle, the haunting air of the Last Post, fading away on its last long even note. So midnight came and the Reveille of the New Year. Another arch was completed; another begun.

IV

I saw work in many stages of development as we continued our journey beyond Nigeria. At Kimpese in the Congo it was only blueprints and the allotted site of land. Now the leprosarium is built, and is to specialize particularly in orthopaedic work in association with the Institut Medical Evangelique. In Ruanda-Urundi at Nyankanda I saw a young leprosarium going through the throes of growing pains, with already over seven hundred in-patients, their number far outstripping the pace of building work. The years since then have seen the erection of many more cottages and of a fine church, and the building-up of a more comprehensive staff.

In Tanganyika we visited, among other leprosy settlements, the old Home at Makutupora, and talked over proposals which in time became plans for a new settlement with modern medical and agricultural facilities. The old Home was originally merely a "leper dump" before the first world war. Then, when the British became the Mandatory Power, the Australian C.M.S. came to have a concern for it and our Mission was able to provide, especially from its friends in Ireland and Australia, more adequate buildings. But the site remained an extremely unsuitable one, straggling up the side of the Rift Valley in an area where there is almost chronic water shortage, and frequent food shortage in consequence. A loving work was engaged in for many deeply needy patients, but under difficulties. So when we visited Makutupora, Bishop Stanway and Dr. H. W. Hannah—the missionary son of Mr. H. J. Hannah, who was the founder of the Australian Auxiliary of the Mission—discussed with me the possibility of our two Missions becoming partners in establishing a really progressive piece of work on a good site, the Australian C.M.S. providing medical missionary personnel and we standing behind the project financially. A site with abundant water is not easy to find in Central Tanganyika and Dr. Hannah motored literally thousands of miles to find it. At last two hundred acres were found. Delays followed over purchase and water rights to draw from a great new dam which has recently been built. But now as I write the plans are all approved, material is being collected, and building work should have begun before these words go into print. As soon as is practicable the patients from Makutupora will be transferred and a new fuller life will open up for them, and the settlement will become the hub of a radiating out-patient work at village centres. It is particularly valuable that at a time when Tanganyika is moving forward through increasing self-govern-

W CHURCHES AT AFRICAN LEPROSY HOMES

See pages 175-177

Right: *Ongino, Uganda*

Left: *Rivers, Isoba, Nigeria*

Right: *Itesio, Kenya*

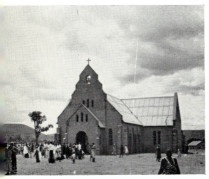

Left: *Nyankanda, Ruanda-Urundi*

Right: *Makete, Tanganyika*

Left: A patient makin
specially fitted shoe

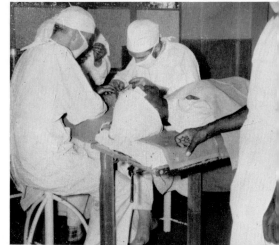

Right: Dr. Fritschi performing
an orthopaedic operation

Below: Some of the Patients' Cottages
(cf. photographs facing p. 45)

ment to full responsibility there should be an evidence
such as this of international Christian goodwill. It is a
happy and significant fact that Dr. Hannah is himself
one of the first elected members of the Legislative Council and speaks with great respect of the Chief Minister,
Julius Nyerere, a devout Christian. "I have little doubt
that history will place Julius Nyerere among the very
great," he has written. Tanganyika's planned progress,
arch by arch, across the bridge from backwardness and
colonialism to independence and prosperity, is a matter
for much thanksgiving. And it is quite certain that
the Christian missionary movement in Tanganyika and
other ill-developed lands has played an important part
in helping them forward to fullness of life. Especially
perhaps in lands where individual life has been held
cheap have the activities year after year of Christ-
inspired compassion helped build the bridge from
bondage to true liberty.

While there were these new enterprises to help forward in Congo, Ruanda-Urundi and Tanganyika, there
were also older ones in which we could see the great
progress made over the arches of the years. There
was, for instance, the work at Kumi, which really
began in 1928, when a deeply Christian doctor in
the Uganda Medical Service, Dr. C. A. Wiggins,
started six small out-patient clinics for giving the chaulmoogra oil treatment to the Teso people. I sat on one
stool and Onesimus Busimo faced me on another in the
dispensary at the Kumi Children's Leprosy Home as
he told me of beginnings. Onesimus, dignified and now
grey-haired, was the senior dispenser. Over his gown
he wore a badge with the single word Mpereza upon
it. He had trained at the great C.M.S. hospital at

173

Mengo, Kampala; and "Mpereza"—"I Serve"— is its motto. Onesimus was serving under Dr. Wiggins in 1928 and remembered well the foundation of the first clinic of all at Kakusi, where I was later to see the roofless, now tumble-down building in which it was housed. Soon the clinics revealed the considerable numbers of children who had already contracted the disease in their infected family surroundings, and that pointed to the next step—the establishment of (so far as I know) the first sanatorium in the world exclusively for children with leprosy. Our Mission promised the support of the first one hundred children; and that support has continued and increased ever since. For many years Miss Margaret Laing "reigned" there. Onesimus became her "prime minister", and the little kingdom she created among the four hundred children was an outstanding witness of Christian concern. "She used to mix the cement with her own hands," said Onesimus to me, "to make sure it was right." That showed her quality. In 1935 work for adult patients at Ongino, six miles away, was added to the children's work, and it was not until 1948 that Miss Laing retired. She had completed her arches of the years, from which others were to build on into the future.

This building-on from earlier beginnings has been progressive in an all-round way. The coming of Dr. Maurice and Mrs. Lea was a gift of God to the work. The call to foreign missionary service could only be answered by Dr. Lea when his children had been educated. Then, laying aside a prosperous practice in England, these two joyously, and with the eagerness of youth, went out to Kumi. Dr. Lea, side by side with an African, was ordained deacon and then priest soon after he reached Uganda, and has engaged in one of those pieces of work in which the spiritual and physical commingle and become one. At about the same time that Dr. Lea went to Uganda Dr. Kinnear Brown became the Government Leprosy Officer. He had been a missionary many years earlier, working in Nigeria and being the first doctor at Uzuakoli, from whom Dr. Davey took over in 1936, when Dr. Brown was compelled to return for some years to England. Now the opportunity came for him to return to Africa, and he brought to Uganda the wide vision of a network of village centres, which always characterized the Uzuakoli enterprise. So it was that Dr. Lea was able to offer ready co-operation with Government in developing voluntary segregation villages for patients who were contagious : these villages also becoming the district leprosy clinics. I was able with Dr. Lea to visit two of the four villages already constructed, including the one at Kakusi, which immediately adjoined the site of Dr. Wiggins' first clinic in 1928. It was only begun in 1955; beautifully laid out, very simple and clean; a centre for public health work; good farming of a hundred and eighty acres by the patients; and an evangelistic centre. I was able to stand outside the dispensary, turning my eyes first to the ruins which symbolized the faith thirty years ago to arise and build; and then to the new village which symbolized the modern and much wider campaign now engaged in, the older order changing and gladly yielding place to new.

It was at Ongino that I also saw, if only in prospect, a similar advance in the worship and witness of the staff and the Christian patients. At the end of the men's hospital ward was a roofed-over platform where,

175

day by day, the dressings of patients living in cottages were done, and where treatment was given. On the Sunday this platform was used for worship, in the absence of a church building. It was not in the least satisfactory, with the sun pouring down on the iron roof, and the hot wind blowing in. On the Sunday I was there Dr. Lea, just before the end of the service, was urgently called into the adjoining ward to minister to a dying man. The physician of bodies was also the physician of souls. He took me along afterwards to the site for the House of Prayer. He was full of enthusiasm and aroused it in others. "I want to pick your brains" was his favourite opening gambit in conversation to get his hearer interested in whatever new project occupied him, and in which he hoped to secure an ally. "I want to pick your brains about this church building. Now what do you think about its orientation? And what about its main features? The patients and we of the staff are clearing the ground, as you see, and the patients breaking up stones." I was quite ready to be enthused, for it is part of our Mission's joy to help in fostering the worship of any Home with which it is linked. It was therefore a happiness here, and at other Stations in Africa we visited, to be the agent of the Mission's purpose in helping to supply financial support for church buildings. As I look back I can thank God that since our visit to Africa our Mission has been a partner in providing church buildings at no less than six of the leprosy stations we visited, now all of them completed —at Rivers in Nigeria; Nyankanda in Ruanda-Urundi; Itesio in Kenya; Kumi in Uganda; Makete in Tanganyika; and Shashemane in Ethiopia. Photographs of some of these appear facing page 172. And from all these Stations come reports of the way in which this international sharing in the work of the universal Christian Church has led to real spiritual enrichment.

Later in our Uganda tour we were to be present at the twenty-fifth anniversary of the building of an earlier church. This was at Bunyonyi, that lovely "Lake of the Little Birds" on which is the small island Bwama, once the haunt of witch-doctors, where now there stands the Leprosy Home and Hospital. At the extreme south of Uganda, lying between enclosing hills, shines the lake like an oval mirror, its edge fringed with blue and pink water lilies. It must have been a great day for Dr. Sharpe of the Ruanda Mission when he found here the site he was looking for—an island exquisitely situated, empty after the police had driven out the witch-doctors who lived there, and still feared because of the evil spirits which might linger unseen among the trees. Leprosy sufferers from the district had come to him at his general hospital some miles away. There was clearly a great need to pioneer in leprosy work. And here was a site which had been a haunt of evil and fear to be transformed into a dwelling of love and life. The Mission to Lepers from the commencement gave its support to the project. And beginning amid the wild tangle of undergrowth Dr. Sharpe set to work to build what has become a charming colony free, by reason of the hilly contour of the island, from the drabness of set-square-planning, and where in place of the dark witchcraft of evil and superstition the love and skill of Christian medical service have brought life and light.

The church building—Emmanuel Church—stands on a ridge of the hilly island, and from which one can look away to the patients' cottages, the hospital wards, the nurses' house, the school, and across a short distance of water to another tiny island on which the present doctor, Dr. Parry, lives. On the morning of the anniversary a pale lavender haze made the whole scene ethereally lovely; and then the sun forced its way through and the sky became a brilliant blue, every colour of tree and building, bird and flower, shining in splendour. The drums kept up their insistent call to worship. Visitors from the mainland arrived in a variety of boats. Officials were there; neighbouring chiefs; discharged patients; the new Bishop of Uganda; five hundred and fifty patients, some men in overcoats, others in European suits, others in long *rigas*; the women with bright patchwork shawls over their best and brightest dresses; the children with shining, excited faces. The great word *Likiga*—God is with us—confronted us, and told us that we did not gather to worship an absentee Creator. A communion service was first held. Then the church filled and flowed over for the great thanksgiving service. It had been gloriously decorated with madonna and blue waterlilies, both of which grow in wild profusion by the lakeside. And there was another glory in the beauty of men and women re-made, made new in Christ, offering their praise for the great things done through the ministry of the years. It was appropriate that the offerings were allotted to help in the cost of a translation of the New Testament into Lunyankoli, the dialect of the people in this area. At present an edition is used in Lunyaruanda, not so near to the people's speech. Many of the ex-patients have been the ones to take word of the Christian Gospel into scattered districts for the first time. In some cases this has led to the establishment of Christian congregations. Here was another instance where God "chose the weak things of the world, that He might put to shame the things that are strong."

V

In the course of our Africa journey we saw leprosy work being engaged in with equal devotion by Englishmen, Scotsmen, Australians, Canadians, Danes, Americans, and Africans of different countries. We worshipped at Leprosy Homes with Anglicans, Baptists, Presbyterians, Methodists, Moravians. We also worshipped with those who served in interdenominational missions and where the problems of determining a church order are having to be faced. Two of the interdenominational missions with which our Mission co-operates are the Africa Inland Mission and the Sudan Interior Mission. And this account of Africa work must, by reason of limits of space, close with references to one enterprise of the A.I.M. and one of the S.I.M. which we visited. I choose these because they illustrate something of the tenacity of purpose and unselfishness of spirit and amplitude of faith of the pioneers who have been the instruments of God's purposes through the years.

Away in the N.W. corner of Uganda we visited an upland station called Kuluva. There we met the "Kuluva Family Williams". There are a number of great family traditions in missionary annals. Usually it is a case of succession from parents to children. But at Kuluva two doctor brothers are at work, and it is their father and mother who have joined them. After service as a surveyor with the Kenya Government, and having helped his sons through their medical course, Mr. and Mrs. Williams went to assist their sons. Technical skill

179

and grace of spirit have been their splendid contribution. I was able to see the fascinating work which Dr. Ted and Dr. Peter Williams have established with the help of their wives and parents. Old Father Williams and his two sons are extraordinarily practical men. Building work, motor engineering, watch repairing, electrical work, making of wireless sets, are all added to the direct medical work. And everything is done "on a shoe string." Never have I seen so much done at such little cost. It sounds fantastic but it is true that £5,000 built the general hospital, the first buildings of the leprosarium, five European staff houses and several African ones, and the church. The hospital included electrical installation, telephonic intercommunication, X-ray equipment. Our guest room had a bathroom attached, with taps "H and C". True, the bath had been hollowed out of a tree trunk and painted white, and the water came from just outside the door where large old oil cans had been filled with water, one of them with a wood fire burning underneath. But no dusty and tired traveller could have wished for more comfort as he turned on the hot tap and lay full length in the long bath.

I recall the Secretary of the A.I.M. ringing me up, and then coming along to our headquarters to tell me of the proposal for a leprosarium at Kuluva. Already the A.I.M. had a general hospital at Arua begun by Dr. Ted Williams. Now Government had asked the co-operation of the Mission in leprosy work to meet the need in the north west part of Uganda, both by helping in the establishment of small local Government leprosy villages, and by starting a central mission leprosarium. A site eight miles from Arua was available. Our Mission's financial aid was invited and it was glad to be able to make provision for two Australian nurses, and to help over the buildings and maintenance. Provision for the dispensary building came about in a very interesting way. A splendid, quite poor, little lady in Adelaide, Australia, Mrs. Parker, was absolutely crippled with arthritis. I can see again my wife carrying her in a blanket from a car to the hall when she was determined to attend a meeting. She thereafter conceived the idea of starting a "Birthday Club", and carried through her project, beginning with friends she knew, with such success that in two or three years enough money was raised by the birthday gifts of those who had moved on to another arch of the years, to provide for the dispensary building—and later for various equipment. Mrs. Parker's own woeful crippling did not drive her in upon herself but made her more sympathetic with the needs of others. A notable example.

The final station we visited in Africa was at Shashemane in Ethiopia, where the Sudan Interior Mission is at work. It was only four years old when we made our visit but the arch of each year had been a broad one, enabling extraordinary progress to be made. Towards the initial buildings American Leprosy Missions gave substantially, and The Mission to Lepers has since helped over a number of fresh projects—the church, the crèche, the carpentry school and so on. But Dr. Thompson, who was in charge, said to me, "The need at our leprosy station at Dessie, only just beginning, is greater than ours. We now have sources of income which I will show you; so can you give any recurring help there?" Our Mission is therefore now more especially involved in the Dessie leprosarium further north, which we did not visit, and which is doing a fine pioneering work among a

Muslim people—never an easy task.

Dr. Thompson, before the Shashemane work began, had had very close association with His Imperial Majesty Haile Selassie, who sent him on several missions, including three to India. This association was of immense help, and His Majesty from the beginning showed great interest in the new enterprise and opened it in 1952. From the leprosarium has developed a general hospital (a reversal of the usual order) and this helps to finance the leprosy work. For instance, the fees from X-ray examinations pay for the X-ray photographs of the leprosy patients' hands and feet. Another source of income for the leprosarium was a Tree Nursery, young plants of good stock finding a ready sale. A coffee plantation was just being laid out. Crippled patients looked after "pedigree" poultry, and a regular income was coming in from one-day-old chicks. There was also some excellent farming and vegetable cultivation. Over four hundred of the patients, the uncrippled ones, were able to live in their own home-built cottages. The other buildings had been erected with great economy and technical skill, and were a great pleasure to see. In all there were some six hundred in-patients and a similar number of out-patients. The whole enterprise, with an adequate staff of missionaries, and with Ethiopians being trained carefully for positions of responsibility, had an air of freshness and efficiency and friendliness. I think it is difficult to overestimate a work of this kind in a land which has been through bitter years of foreign domination, with its king in exile. This bridge of compassion spans the gulf of suspicion, fear and hurt pride, which is the legacy of Ethiopia's recent history, and brings in their place enduring fellowship.

VI

A good deal has been written in this book (on pp. 93-108) about the dramatic young enterprise at Hong Kong, by which an uninhabited island in 1951 was turned into an Isle of Happy Healing. After my visit in 1954 I was able to return in 1958, and I saw something of the remarkable progress made in the interval. Ezekiel has a strange passage describing his vision of the re-built temple at Jerusalem. In it he writes of the various gates into the courtyards of the Lord, and that "there were narrow windows to the arches"; small look-outs from within. It is only possible to peep through narrow windows in the arches of the years and take fleeting glimpses of the progress made each year between 1954 and 1958. In 1955 we see further cottages built, largely by Government's help, for another one hundred and sixty patients; three more staff quarters; a fine tuberculosis ward a little distance from the main hospital; and a pier down in the bay. It was also in this year that the first Scout Troop was inaugurated and the island became a training centre for medical students of the Hong Kong University. In 1956 there was the construction of a large concrete arch dam up in the hills to ensure a fuller water supply for the larger number of patients—now over five hundred. This project owed its initiative to Mr. O. Skinner, then the Chairman of the ever-active Hong Kong Auxiliary, and its planning to Brigadier G. B. Gifford Hull, an expert in dam construction. Much of the funds needed came from the generous friends of the Rotary Club in Kowloon. The first Guide Troop on the island was enrolled in this year. It was also the year when the work suffered the loss by death of a great friend and helper, the architect Mr. G. A. V. Hall, who had voluntarily prepared all the major plans of the various buildings on the island and given great attention to their execution. He said that his work for sufferers from leprosy, who were held captive in the grip of a great enemy, was his thankoffering for the survival and eventual release of himself and his wife from long captivity in World War II, when the enemy overran Hong Kong.

In 1957 more staff quarters went up, more roads were built, including a bridge over one of them. Permanent huts for livestock were erected and a store for dangerous goods. This was the year when the W.H.O. Regional Conference for the Western Pacific visited the island, and found much to learn. Afterwards it formally recommended that all designated for leprosy work in the East should go to the island for training, not only for the knowledge to be obtained, but "to absorb if possible something of the spirit of dedication which animates the work."

The year 1958 saw the opening by the Governor, Sir Robert Black, K.C.M.G., O.B.E., of a considerable extension to the main hospital block, with two spacious new wards, and the introduction of a campaign of Reconstructive Surgery, led by Dr. Douglas Harman, after teaching visits from the plastic surgeon, Dr. William White, from the U.S.A., and the orthopædic surgeon, Dr. Paul Brand, from India.

As I crossed to the island I noticed immediately a change of outline at one point. The sharp edge of the bare hills was now softened and fluffy, for the afforestation work was beginning to show results as thousands of pine trees grew from seedlings into saplings, which will in time provide abundant fuel. And when I arrived I was able to land on the 175 feet pier on which there waited long lines of welcoming patients. Among them were the Scouts and Guides, the Guides having been singularly honoured a few months previously by a visit from Lady Baden-Powell, who insisted on coming across a very choppy sea in bad weather. From these Guides she received a gift of their embroidery, a tablecloth, which she asked to be allowed to present as the very first gift for the World Guide Centre, shortly to be erected in England.

It was, as to all visitors, a heartening experience to move among so alert and purposeful a community. Sometimes it is said that the modern man has no idea of where he is going; it is just motion without motive. Here, however, everyone appeared to be full of purpose. Even the hospital patients didn't regard their time in bed as one for sheer lazing. Wheeled tables were drawn over many of the beds, and patients awaiting or recovering from surgery busily engaged in embroidery work, at which the men as well as the women attained a very high standard. I watched with fascination one woman, the fingers of whose right hand were in plaster, and whose left had clawed fingers, laboriously holding her needle between the bent little and third fingers (the only ones of any use) and working away at an embroidered towel. She appeared quite radiantly happy. The first patient I happened to see being examined in the treatment room was a man having his eyes attended to. He was then living in one of the cottages, but attending hospital as an out-patient. When he had been admitted, however, he lay for long in one of the hospital

185

beds, at first a very desperate man. He had thrown himself out of the third storey of a building in Kowloon when life had become intolerable, because of neighbours' fears and the relentless progress of his disease. But he failed to kill himself. His jaw and leg were broken and he was in a terrible mess. After some treatment in Hong Kong he was brought to the Isle of Happy Healing. Care and love renewed his body and soul. Now he had charge of a little workshop in the basement of the hospital where he was able to follow his trade of cobbler in making specially shaped shoes for crippled feet. Story after story can be told of what this once empty island has meant in bringing new life to the broken.* And one of the secrets has been in giving to each patient a new purpose, a new sense of partnership. A definite task is allotted to all except the very ill. Even the blind patients are found useful jobs. A blind ex-carpenter patient still plays his part by doing the sand-papering of the wood which is used to make the attractive book-rests and paper-knives and trays which the patients turn out.

This partnership is not only between staff and patients. It includes the active partnership of many friends in Hong Kong. While I paid my visit an inspector of the Hong Kong Electric Company was giving a week of his holiday to help supervise the installation of a new generator. A married lady who had been a physiotherapist came over each week to give her services; a leading dentist took on the care of the patients' teeth, sailing over in his yacht and giving time at the weekends. The Hong Kong Auxiliary and perhaps especially the ladies' section known as the Marianne Reichl Group continues

* See *Beyond the Bitter Sea*. Published by The Mission to Lepers. Price 2s. in the British Isles.

to be amazingly active. I don't know how many regular
working parties they have, but quite a number. Their
efforts up to the time I write have resulted in a total of
over £28,000 help to the work. Sir Robert Black was
right when, in his speech at the opening of the hospital
extension block, he referred to the work as an "Adventure in Co-operation".

It was my privilege to be present at a gathering of
staff and patients for which there was a double reason.
One was to welcome the Mission's Chairman of Council,
Mr. Bernard Studd, and Mrs. Studd; the other to bid
farewell to Dr. and Mrs. Fraser, who were shortly to
leave after a magnificent piece of pioneer work.

Dr. Fraser not unnaturally found it hard to speak.
He had listened to many tributes and received the tokens
of the patients' and the staff's gratitude. Briefly he
ranged over the arches of the years, speaking to different
groups in turn. He spoke of the different aspects of the
work which impressed visitors most, "but what impresses
all is the way in which staff and patients work together
as one team. Best of all the gifts you have presented to
me is the knowledge that you will support those who
follow me with the same loyalty you have shown to me."

It was a very moving occasion, lightened by touches
of humour from Dr. Fraser's first senior helper, Mr.
Lau, who described the sea-sickness of the first pioneer
patients as they came across to the empty island, told us
of how Dr. Fraser, his mind so engrossed in the work,
once put on Mr. Lau's trousers by mistake, and on
another occasion went and had his hair cut without a
cent to pay for it!

While I was on the island Dr. Paul Brand was also
there, teaching refinements of surgical techniques to Dr.

Harman and his assistants. He was helped by the fact that the hospital now has the finest X-ray records anywhere of patients' hands and feet. Altogether the medical and surgical work, with the British and Chinese staff doctors, the British, Canadian and Chinese nurses, and with voluntary visiting doctors, especially Dr. Skinsnes and Dr. Sturton, was of outstanding quality; together with it, and at its heart, was the Christian Church, with its manifold activities radiating from The Lord Wills Church, where I was privileged to be present both at a baptismal and a communion service.

As I left on the motor launch I stood at the stern waving to a company standing on the pier. I was not the only one to be leaving. For at the prow stood another passenger waving. He was in a neat grey Chinese suit, and he was a healed and newly discharged patient. How had he come? In fear and despair? But now he was an "ordinary" man again, though a radically different man from the one he had been before leprosy attacked him. For now he went back to life in the community not only with returned health but with a new knowledge of God as he had come to know Him in Christ through the services of His disciples. How appropriate that the uninhabited Nun Island was re-named Hay Ling Chau —The Isle of Happy Healing!

VII

Since the earlier chapters of this book were written much has taken place in the development of the Mission's leprosy work in India and Burma; less in Pakistan. A good deal of this development has been of an undramatic character—here a little, there a little. Among building projects have been the hospital block at Poladpur (a Home referred to on pp. 120 to 122), notable for the fact that, under the working direction of Dr. V. P. Das (for he himself turned workman) it was erected entirely by the patients;* the hospital block at Bankura; and the orthopædic wing at Purulia, also largely built by the patients' labour, with its X-ray equipment, treatment rooms and operating theatre. The buildings of the Children's Sanatorium at Faizabad (p. 82) have been completed, including the fine school and assembly hall; and a large wing for boys with leprosy at the Champa Home has been built. In Burma the war-damaged Homes at Mandalay and Moulmein have been extensively repaired and improved, and in particular the patients at Moulmein have built entirely with their own hands a new hospital block. These are some of the building projects completed, but there has also been a constant effort to march in step with medical developments, to increase village treatment work, and to bring the benefits of preventive and remedial exercises to affected hands and feet. It is, however, only possible to refer to two significant advances, one in the south and one in the north of India.

The development in the north only stems from the Mission's work, and is not a part of it. I referred in an earlier chapter (pp. 82 to 87) to the quite remarkable courage and love of two healed patients Sri Bijai Nath Tripathi and Sri Ratnaswamy, who together established a new leprosy enterprise at Gorakhpur. When I visited Faizabad in 1959 Dr. Chandy kindly arranged for his "All Friends Day" to be held while my wife and I were

* See *Two Pioneers at Poladpur,* by A. Donald Miller. Published by The Mission to Lepers. Price 1s. in the British Isles.

there. It was celebrated with the usual enthusiasm, elephants and Police Band complete. Among ex-patients who returned for this "old school-tie" occasion was one who is now an evangelist, another who is a constable working in the C.I.D., another who was taking full training as a nurse, others who had their own farms, and some who had joined staffs in leprosy clinics. There were also Tripathi and Ratnaswamy. It was an inspiration to have a long talk with them, together with Dr. Chandy, who, under God, had been the one to inspire their faith and action. They were able to tell me of the Home and Hospital they had established at Gorakhpur, with its good buildings, partly built from help from the Gandhi Memorial Fund, and where an obviously good work was being done. Later, in a very gracious personal letter from Tripathi-ji he wrote this striking passage, which takes on its full significance when one remembers how he first came to Faizabad, as has been described on p. 85 :—

"Since the establishment of our institution (at Gorakhpur) in 1951, sixteen leprosy clinics have come into being through our direct help, and I feel pride in the fact that the light of healing which has been passed on to these centres was the one originally drawn from the Mission Home at Faizabad. In all humility, we do praise Him for having given us the responsibility of being co-workers with Him in imparting health and life to those afflicted with leprosy."

As we travelled to the south of India we passed from the white glare of the dry, blanched countryside of the sunlit winter in the north. We came to the vivid emerald green of rice fields still to be harvested, and the silhouette of various kinds of palm trees against blazing sunset skies; the bright colours of women's saris, the genial warm air. Our main visit was to the Schieffelin Leprosy Research Sanatorium at Karigiri, near Vellore. I have told on pp. 54 to 57 of the beginnings of this Sanatorium, and of how in December 1953 the first main buildings were dedicated while my wife and I were able to be present, even though they were not entirely ready for occupation. Now we returned in 1959 to a centre positively humming with activity, and already with a fine record of work to its credit. All looked so different from the bare site over which I had walked in 1948, and which appeared most unpromising, but which had to be accepted because of failure to secure anything nearer to the Vellore Christian Medical College, in association with which the sanatorium functions. Flowering shrubs and trees shone out against the grey stone buildings; roads cut through hitherto stony wastes took one to the well-planned patients' cottages, or to the hospital and administration block, or to the staff houses at the foot of Elephant Hill, or to the semi-permanent community building which at present serves as church, library, school and recreation hall. The number of inpatients is deliberately limited to 150, because of the special nature of the work, which would be spoilt if quantity interfered with quality. But that limit creates constant embarrassment. On the very first afternoon we were there a man with very advanced and untreatable leprosy was dumped nearby and left. He was quite unsuitable for the special work of the sanatorium, yet quite unable to take himself off again. (Fortunately a day or two later it was possible to make other arrangements for him and take him away in the car in which we travelled on to Vadathorasalur). And on that same first afternoon, going round the men's surgical ward with Dr. Fritschi, we came to the bed of a very ill man, with the disease far gone, who had somehow made the journey all the way from Bombay, having heard of Karigiri's growing fame. He just had to be given a place for a time, at the cost of excluding some more suitable patient. These are illustrations of the embarrassment to which the staff is constantly exposed. It is always dangerous to excel!

Apart from the one hundred and fifty in-patients, who are ordinarily admitted because they are suitable for the particular research work in which the doctors and physiotherapist engage, there is an almost wildly popular out-patient clinic. The site is an inconveniently remote one, a mile back from the main road, and near no village, but the clinic is immensely popular. On foot, on bicycles, in bullock carts the patients appear in their hundreds, and each one receives that careful individual attention which has the inevitable result of making the clinic more and more popular. When we were there there was a regular attendance of 2,000, with 3,000 on the roll. This number has since increased to over 4,000!

It is in this situation of the ever-increasing pressure of popularity which first-class work brings that the work goes forward. The two resident doctors when we were there were Dr. E. P. Fritschi, who combined the offices of superintendent, spiritual leader and surgeon, and Dr. C. K. Job, pathologist and physician. Mr. David Ward was the resident physiotherapist and Miss B. A. McKay the one missionary nurse. There were, of course, numerous visiting physicians and surgeons, led by our Director of Orthopædic work, Dr. Paul Brand, of whose astonishing work I have written on pp. 41 to 47. On the afternoon of our arrival Mrs. (Dr.) Margaret Brand was holding her eye clinic in the little black room along one of the hospital corridors. I remember how as I watched her she touched the cornea of a patient's eye, and got no response from normally so sensitive a spot. It was another case of "too late", for nerve damage had already done its deadly work. But for others help can be given, though nerve involvement of the eye by leprosy is still a very serious and intractable condition. Other visiting physicians and surgeons from the College come with their special qualifications, and doctors who are training at Karigiri are able to play a very useful part as temporary house doctors. Altogether, with slender resources for so great a task, a quite enthralling piece of constructive work is being engaged in, with special lines of research being followed by individual doctors and the physio-therapist. These cannot be outlined here, but they cover a surprisingly wide range, and make their substantial contribution to a fuller understanding of the disease itself, of its direct treatment, and of the consequences and proper care of neural damage.

There was something thrilling in being taken round the hospital wards and seeing situations of human despair or extremity being met with a combination of skill, patience, and good humour. I went with Dr. Fritschi on his surgical ward round; plaster of paris abounded, each cast with the date fingered into it, so that there should be no doubt as to when it was due for removal. Hands and feet, hitherto regarded as useless, were now being marvellously repaired by the operations of tendon transplantation which Dr. Brand had first introduced, the refinements or range of these operations developing almost month by month. Some faces were a criss-cross patchwork of elastoplast bandages covering bone-grafts

193

N

that were making new noses which before had been sunk. Other patients were in the process of growing new eyebrows in place of those destroyed by the disease—a rather tricky and laborious process of transplantation which, if not carefully done, can lead to the hairs growing in the wrong direction or, more amusingly, taking on an exaggerated activity, to the joy of men patients who feel that this declares them to be very much "he-men"! In one bed was a man, Superamanian, who had to make a difficult choice. He had been a professional clarinet player. "Your twisted fingers are in a condition by which I can either enable you by operation to bring them tightly together so that you can eat with your hands (the traditional way), or else draw them apart so that you can play your clarinet," said Dr. Fritschi to him. "But I can't do both." Superamanian chose the latter alternative; and for eating he was provided with special adjusted "spoons". In telling me of this instrumentalist Dr. Fritschi also pointed me to another man, of cheery countenance, who liked to entertain other patients with his songs, and, in the absence of the traditional drum with which to accompany himself, used his enamel rice plate as a kind of tambourine.

On the medical side Dr. C. K. Job was engaged in a careful pathological study of diseased parts, whether of nerve tissues or of bones. The delicacy of the instruments, and the complexity of the technical details of study, awe the mere layman. But it is by the trained and continuing observations of minute details that clues are found, one by one as in a detective story, which gradually build up knowledge. Dr. Job was able to combine the direct medical care of his patients with the work of his laboratory. Always the rising numbers of patients seeking medical care tended to squeeze out time for leisurely laboratory study, but Dr. Job endeavoured to arrive at a fair balance.

In the orthopædic workshop Mr. Ward and the patients who assist him were wrestling with the problems of " Boots, boots, boots, movin' up and down again". "The more I see of feet," said Mr. Ward to me as he was cutting away at the horny skin under a man's big toe, "the more fascinated I become. I've always liked hands, but feet, you know, struck me as rather ugly. But now as I work upon them I find they fascinate me." All sorts of devices were being tried out to prevent pressure falling on to parts of the feet weakened by disease; a Chinese, India-domiciled, patient was rendering superbly good help in the making of footwear specially adapted for the individual's needs. There is still a long way to go in developing this side of the work, but for each one who is helped the care given makes a tremendous difference.

One was conscious as one saw various facets of the work at Karigiri that one was in the presence of a great confrontation between physical and often spiritual despair on the one hand, and on the other of dedicated minds and lives using their skills and their inventiveness and their spiritual faith to win a victory not only for those in their immediate care, but also for a much wider number, as techniques tested and found to be successful were shared with doctors who came for training, or in a larger way by contributions to medical journals. Here one was in the midst of one of the true battles of life on which all men of goodwill are challenged to engage, the battles not between man and man, but man and the evils which beset him. That is why a good leprosy hospital is always a place of the utmost good cheer, even in the midst of suffering. Here is a war that brings only life and not death.

I was greatly impressed by the way in which involvement in a heavy weight of medical and surgical research work had not resulted in a total absorption in it. It was not forgotten that the man is greater than his disease, and God greater than either. By reason of the fact that the change-over rate of patients is more rapid than in the traditional leprosy Home, there cannot be any established membership of the Christian Church of any size. But there can be, and is, clear proclamation of the Healing Gospel. The services of Christian worship were a focal point in the life of the sanatorium, not only for staff but for ambulatory patients, most of whom looked forward to the Christian services, and participated in them. Much of the human credit for this—though they would be the last to look for it—rested upon two men, one on the staff and one a patient, Dr. Fritschi and Mr. Martin. Dr. Fritschi is himself a Deacon of the Church of South India and hopes one day to engage in study that will lead to his full ordination as a minister of religion to the leprosy patients. He quickly saw the need for a centre for worship, as also for a community centre and school, but he also recognised that he must be content with one building to begin with, and secured help from within India which enabled him to build a very attractive, if only semi-permanent, building for the astonishingly modest sum of Rs. 3,000 or £225. It has a steep thatch roof, on a frame of teak wood, exposed as in a barn. The main supporting pillars are of rough-hewn grey granite, which is fortunately abundant in that stony land. The sides are open, the ends closed. The floor is of pressed mud, with a topping of broken brick and cement. Thus, at little cost, a pleasant commodious centre has been built. In it I saw on a week-day patients using it as a reading room, and others as a school. On the Sunday we joined in the praise of God and when the Holy Communion was celebrated according to the beautiful liturgy of the Church of South India (though we were a bit clumsy in our execution of it), it was notable that the non-Christian patients desired to remain to witness this central act of Christian thanksgiving and spiritual renewal, and sat in reverent silence.

Part of the service was led by Mr. Martin, the Tamil patient who has, with Dr. Fritschi, made so signal a contribution to the spiritual health of the sanatorium. Physically, Mr. Martin's prognosis is not good; he has leprosy in one of its most intractable forms, with frequent painful and wearying reactions, and with poor response to the sulphone and other treatments. So any joy and peace which he has do not come from the buoyancy of returning health. He has also to bear the sorrow of a sensitive man indefinitely separated from his family, his home, and his career as a schoolmaster. Yet he is making a striking contribution in helping the sanatorium to become a centre of new life at its deepest levels. I met him first in his little room in one of the cottages. On the verandah was a table with religious publications in Tamil and English on it. This was his lending library, and sales counter. There were free tracts also. Within the room were other books of his own for devotional use, or reference; Baillie's *Diary of Private Prayer*, William Goudge's *Blessings of Suffering*, and so on. Into this room came other patients to talk over with him, as with a *guru*, the things of the Spirit and the yearnings of the heart. Mr. Martin was engaged in translating into Tamil Philip Loyd's *The Holy Spirit*, at the request of the Superintendent of the Vellore Christian Medical College. A translation of Stephen Neill's *Who is Jesus Christ?* was in the press. He has also translated Amy Carmichael's *The Indian Robin Hood*, J. Edwin Orr's *Full Surrender*, and other books which add to the inadequate number of Christian books circulating in the Tamil language. Mr. Martin arranges Bible classes, morning prayers, a singing practice, and even, I was told, has some students outside for whom he arranges a correspondence course in Bible study. He showed me five large Tamil hymn books he had just received for community use, the gift of a Hindu patient who, on her discharge, had made this thank-offering. Later in my visit I saw him moving among the chattering crowd of waiting out-patients with scripture portions for free distribution, and with Gospels for sale. Such a man is indeed one of God's bridge-builders.

Plans are now being prepared for a permanent House of Prayer, and it is hoped that this will be built in a way and on a site which will make it the clear centre and peak of the sanatorium. I do not feel that the architecture of Christian churches in India has yet quite reached the point where function, tradition, and beauty all blend to make a total offering of the best for the worship and glory of God and the proclamation of His Word. Among the indirect contributions which Mission leprosy hospitals can make is that of providing opportunities for imaginative planning in simple church buildings which is in keeping with the heritage and conditions of the people. It is hoped that at Karigiri such a contribution will be made. In the brief years since the sanatorium received its first patient, solid arches of progress have been built in medical, surgical, and rehabilitation work, and a further one can be achieved if the permanent church building embodies features which will advance the way towards a worthy architecture for Indian places of Christian worship.

VIII

The last of the arches of the years since 1954, to which I am able to make only brief reference, is the VIIth International Congress of Leprology held in Tokyo in November 1958. Five years had elapsed since the Madrid Congress about which I wrote on pages 23-25. The old warriors who were at Madrid—Muir, Wade, Cochrane, Davey, Doull, Ross Innes, Contreras —were still engaged in battle, and they had further, if usually undramatic, advances to report. Only John Lowe was missing; he had crossed the final arch into the life beyond, and must have heard the welcome "Well done . . . " But Dr. Kensuke Mitsuda, who had not been at Madrid, and of whom I wrote on pages 30-31, was present, though well on in his eighties, and he received the ovation he deserved after his sixty years of unbroken service.

Our own Mission's doctors played important parts; Dr. Neil Fraser took the chair at the meetings of the Committee on Classification; and Dr. Paul Brand gave the best set out and delivered lecture of the Congress, watched and listened to with intense interest. He spoke on the Prevention of Deformity and vividly illustrated his theme. To be cured of active leprosy, but with crippled hands and feet, was a Pyrrhic victory. To prevent such crippling was now our greatest challenge, and he showed how this can be done. The last gulf which needed bridging was between healing and rehabilitation. .

I myself worked on the Committee which dealt with Social Aspects of the Disease. This group had a more important rôle than ever before, and it was most significant that our Chairman should be none other than Professor T. N. Jagadisan, whose remarkable story of victory over circumstances I have told on pages 49-52. There could not have been a finer representative of successful rehabilitation, one whose outstanding gifts were wedded to a deep understanding of human need. He pleaded eloquently that scientific knowledge and humane, reasoned, but at the same time passionate social action, should go hand in hand, a "conjunction of scientific adventure and compassionate action which has led to progress in the past and which will lead us to the ultimate conquest over this ancient enemy of mankind". He used a searching quotation from Shakespeare's Twelfth Night:

> In nature there is no blemish but the mind.
> *None can be called deformed, but the unkind:*
> Virtue is beauty . . .

Where better could we close this chapter than there in the Congress Hall, with Jagadisanji in his white homespun Indian attire, the superbly beautiful chrysanthemums cultivated by Japanese patients, and sent as their gift, standing on either side of the platform, and the two hundred delegates from forty-three countries listening to those words? The centuries of unkindness, revealing man's true deformity, were passing away, and the victories of compassionate action were quickly mounting. In a little while all the delegates, religious, social, medical, would be back at their tasks; and in a divided and deformed world they would be taking their part not only in a great task of physical healing but of spiritual reconciliation, for in the building of the bridge of compassion they are surely at work on one of the things which belong unto man's peace.

THE BRIDGE BEYOND

I said in the introduction to this book that while we might join in the building of the Bridge of Compassion there was another bridge, the Bridge of Christ's Passion, which He alone could provide to bring man safely at the last to his true abiding place. After our visit to Korea in 1954 we returned to Japan, and made a visit to the National Leprosarium at Nagashima, an island on the Inland Sea. It is an outstanding institution in very many ways, and after we had seen some of its manifold activities, the paintings of the artist patients, the work of the poetry club, the schools, the hospital wards, the communal kitchens, the gardens, and so on, we went to the Church of the Dawn, Akebonu, where the Christian patients meet for worship. To reach it we had to pass, not over an arch but under one, an arch called in Japanese " The Arch of Believing ". We came to a lovely little building right against the seashore, and overspread with the branches of fragrant, whispering pine trees. We took our places with Dr. Saikawa in the transept for staff and visitors. Already most of the congregation of patients had arrived; they were seated on the floor which was covered with fine rush matting. They waited quietly. Some prayed. At the far end the door opened on to a covered porch. I watched those who were still arriving remove their slippers and enter. One man called Okadu sat down and removed not his slippers but both his artificial legs, and then propelled himself forward with his hands. Some blind patients were led in. Others left their crutches outside and sat down, advancing, feet first, along the floor. I brought greetings from friends in many parts of the world, and especially from those who had had the happiness of helping, together with members of the Japanese Church and other Japanese friends, in the provision of the church building which has gone up since the end of the war. The pastor replied. He is himself a patient. He asked me to return the greetings, and to express the patients' thanks. And then he said that there were four features about the Church at this Leprosarium on the Inland Sea that he would like me to note. " This Church," he said, " is a Fellowship. And first it is a Fellowship with Christ. That is where it begins. He is here with us, and in Him we have life and joy and peace. And then it is a Fellowship with men. The Christians on the staff share with us in our worship; ministers of many places and denominations come to us and bring us teaching; visitors like yourselves come from far parts of the world and represent a worldwide fellowship with us of Christian friends. And, thirdly, it is a growing Fellowship. We began with thirty members when the church was built. Now we are over a hundred. Soon the church will not be large enough to hold us. The message of Christ is drawing in other patients, and its influence spreads through the whole Leprosarium. And, fourthly, we are an evangelistic Fellowship. We prepare our own Christian bulletin. We have our own printing press. We write our testimonies, our poems, our messages. And this bulletin we circulate to the other leprosaria in Japan, and to tuberculosis sanatoria, and to prisons. We want to share with others in need our faith and our hope. Thus we are not a people cut off, even though we spend our days on this island, for we have fellowship with Christ, and with our fellow-men."

As he spoke my eyes fell on a large dark blue glazed pot that stood on the ground between us. In it was a miniature tree trunk, gnarled, twisted, its bark all shed. It might almost have been, one thought, a tree badly deformed with leprosy in its most crippling type. And then I saw that into it there had been grafted a shoot of camellia, which was being nourished by the life imparted to it through that stripped and seemingly dead trunk. I looked at the shining, smooth leaves of the graft and among them I saw buds of the lovely pure white flowers, waiting to open into their full beauty. A whole parable was there; and the truth which it proclaimed was there, too, in the lives of those transformed men and women still to arrive at their full glory. What was the Latin Vulgate version of Isaiah's words about the Messiah, " We did esteem him stricken, smitten of God, and afflicted "? Was it not " Nos vidimus eum quasi leprosum . . ."? *" We beheld him as leprous."* Yet in that tortured and despised Body flowed the very Life of God for man. And by His Passion, His utter self-donation, He became the final Bridge to bring men to their redemption, and flowering, and fullness of life. Beyond the Bridge of Compassion, in the building of which we may by God's grace share, we stand at the last before the Bridge of the Cross which is His alone. And by it He invites us all, whatever our condition, and opens up the Way for us to enter into His Promised Land.

Information regarding the work of The Mission to Lepers may be obtained from any of its offices :—

7 Bloomsbury Square, London, W.C.1 (Head Office); 20 Lincoln Place, Dublin, C.17; 44 Ulsterville Avenue, Belfast, 9; 5 St. Andrew Square, Edinburgh, 2; 7 Royal Bank Place, Glasgow, C.1; Rooms 1101-3, 67 Yonge Street, Toronto, 1; 174 Collins Street, Melbourne, C.1; 43 Mount Eden Road, Auckland; 30 Seventh Avenue, Highlands North, Johannesburg; Purulia, West Bengal, India; P.O. Box 380, Hong Kong.